DIY Guide to Beautiful Wire and Beaded Jewelry Making for Beginners

The Simple Step-by-Step Handbook for Starting Jewelry Crafts at Home

By

Amy Ray

Copyrighted Material

Copyright © 2019 – *Streets of Dream Press*

All Rights Reserved.

No part of this publication may be reproduced, stored in a retrieval system or transmitted in any form or by any means, electronic, mechanical, photocopying, recording or otherwise without the proper written consent of the copyright holder, except brief quotations used in a review.

Published by:

Streets of Dream Press

Streets of Dream Press

Cover & Interior designed

By

Rebecca Floyd

First Edition

Table of Contents

Acknowledgments 4

Introduction 5

Part 1: Wire Art Jewelry 7

Wire Rose Ring 15

Wire Rose Pendant 23

Wire Rose Dangle Earrings 27

Wire Nest Pendant 37

Bead and Wire Studs 48

Part 2: Beaded Jewelry 56

Stackable Separate Beaded Bracelets 58

Beaded Wrap Bracelet 70

Crafting with a Bead Loom 82

Conclusion 94

Acknowledgments

First and foremost, this entire project has been a labor of love for me. I would like to thank several people who inspired me and encouraged me in achieving this dream of finally becoming a published author.

I would like to thank my friend Jamie Swanson, who so graciously helped me photograph the pieces in this book. She has been a loyal and true friend for years. I appreciate her immensely.

I would also like to thank my mom Sarah. She has endured so much as a single mom while raising me. Without her, none of this would be possible.

Last but not least, I would like to thank you, the reader of this publication. I hope this book has helped and inspired you. I hope it helps you tap into your inner creative side.

Happy crafting!

Introduction

Jewelry has always been a part of the human experience. Even in prehistoric times, humans have utilized and worn jewels and jewelry. Alongside the earliest simple tools, humans also made and wore jewelry.

Jewelry and jewels have frequently been used as currency in many cultures around the world. In most societies, a woman's wealth is kept in her jewelry. Jewelry is an investment.

The jewelry we choose to wear is a very personal and deliberate statement about who we are as a person.

The colors, stones, metal, beads, shape, size are all a big factor in its appeal. Assuming it is liked, the question becomes when, where, and for what occasion will it be worn.

Jewelry making is such a fun and practical skill to have for many reasons, but mainly because all the decisions of color, stone, metal, beads, shape, and size are all your own personal decisions to make. The jewelry becomes as custom as possible.

Creating jewelry yourself is a HUGE money saver. For pennies on the dollar, not only can you fill your jewelry box, but also make personalized and beautiful pieces for friends and family. You will always have the perfect gift for any holiday or occasion.

Once you buy a few materials and learn a few basic techniques, the sky's the limit!

Part 1: Wire Art Jewelry

Wire jewelry is not only one of the easiest forms of jewelry to make, but it is also one of the most inexpensive.

There are a few basic tools you will need for almost every project. You can customize the wires you want to work with depending on the needs of the piece.

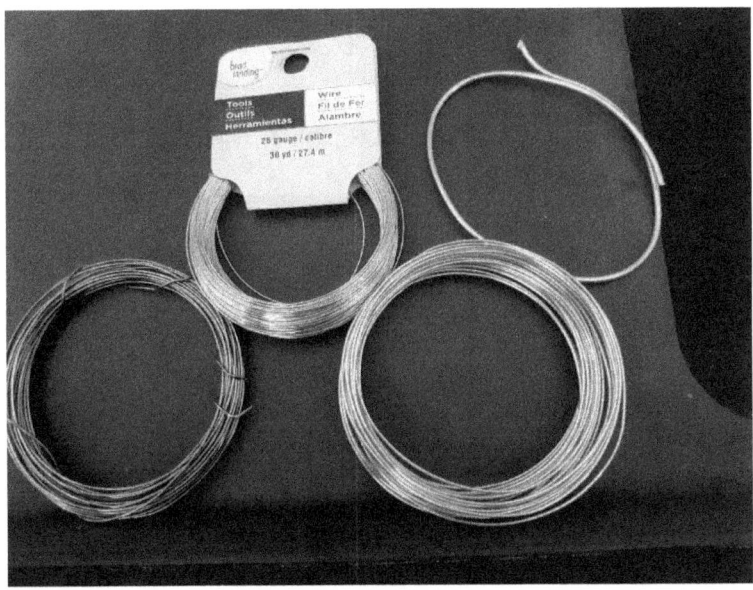

Here you can see the wires I used in these projects that are different metals and different gauges (or thicknesses). They are very inexpensive and sold at many craft or hobby stores.

As for the tools, there are five main ones that almost always come in a set or package.

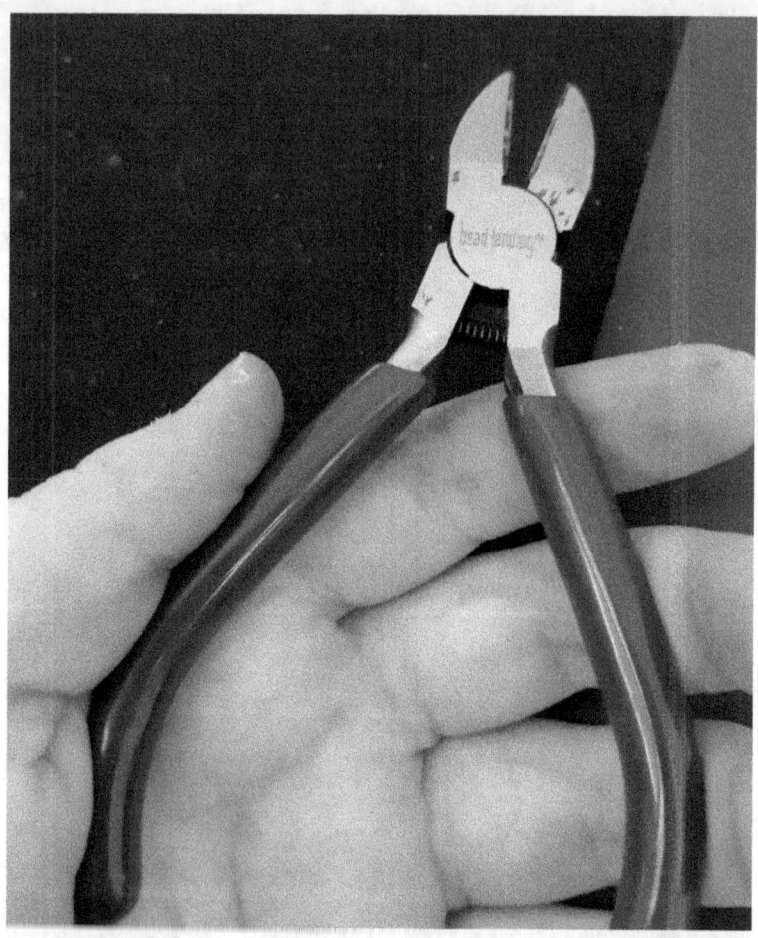

The first tool is a wire cutter. It is crucial for getting close snips on delicate pieces. It does the heavy lifting when a wire is too thick or strong for scissors.

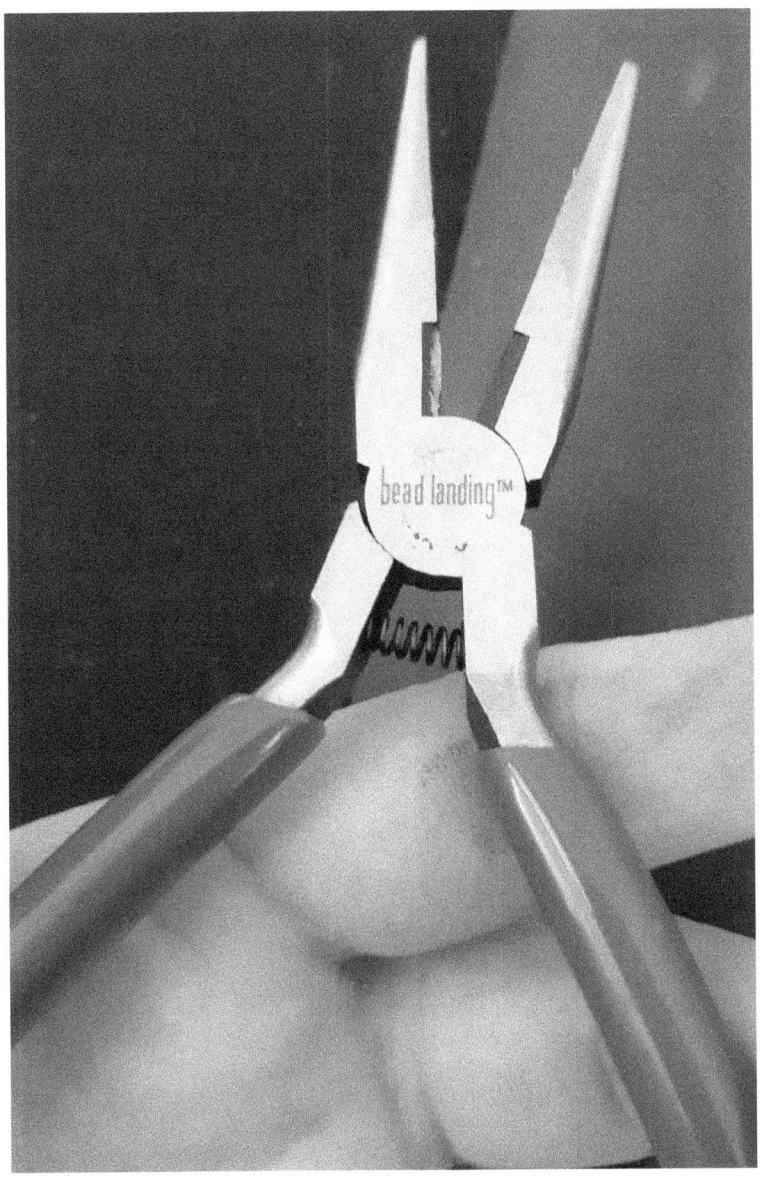

The next tool is a pair of needle nose pliers which come in handy far more times than you can imagine. To be honest, I think almost every artist needs a good pair of needle nose pliers.

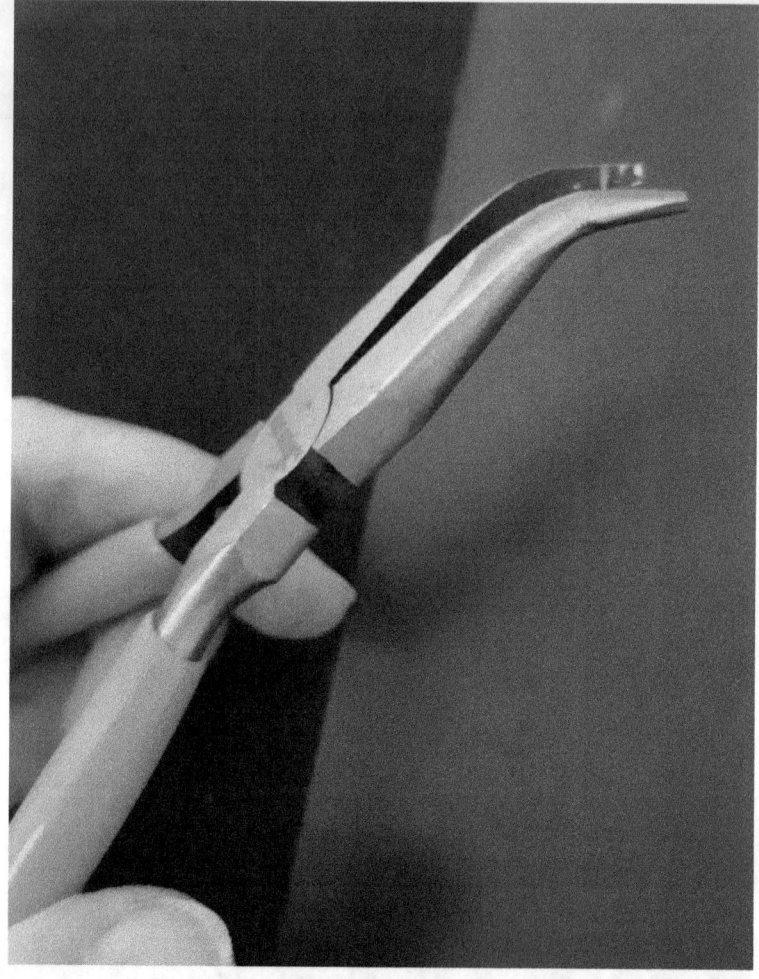

These bent needle nose pliers are very helpful in reaching places where the other ones just will not fit or are not the right angle.

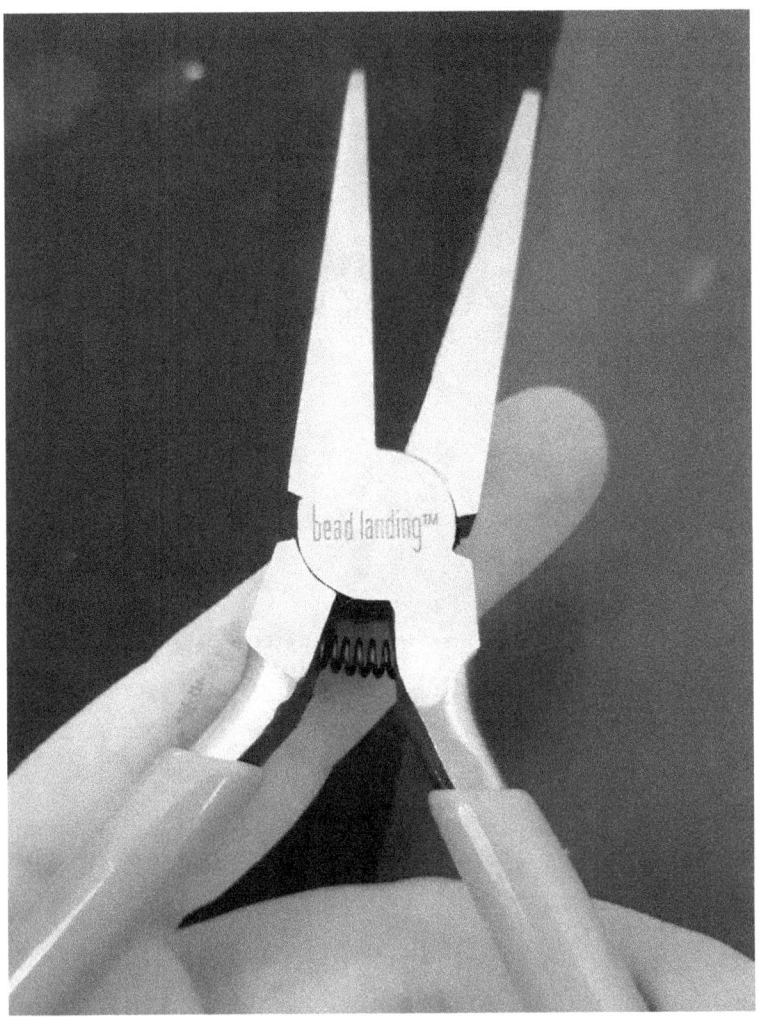

These are called flat nose pliers and are used for gripping and shaping with an angle or for flattening out a bent wire.

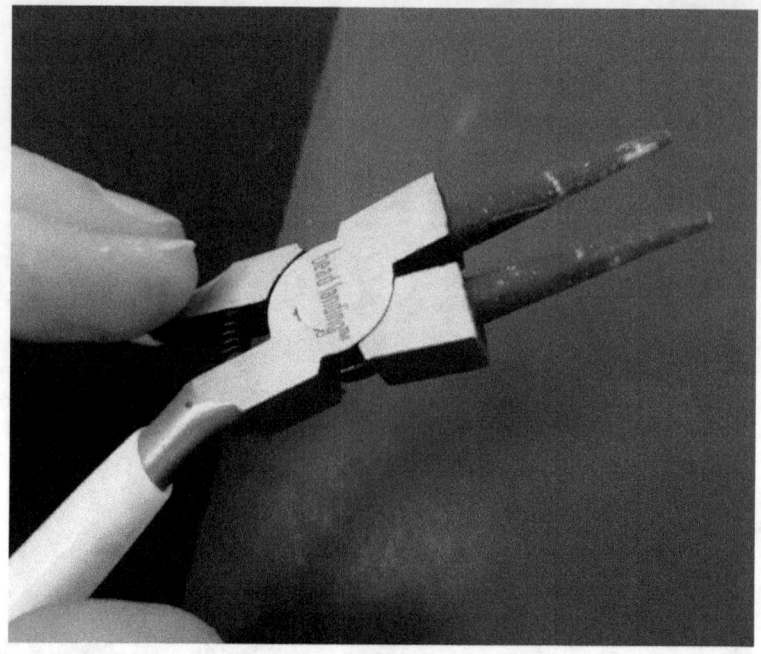

These are called round nose pliers and are used for creating curves and small loops.

The jewelry you can make with these tools is endless.

Here are the examples of the pieces we will be working on in this tutorial.

14

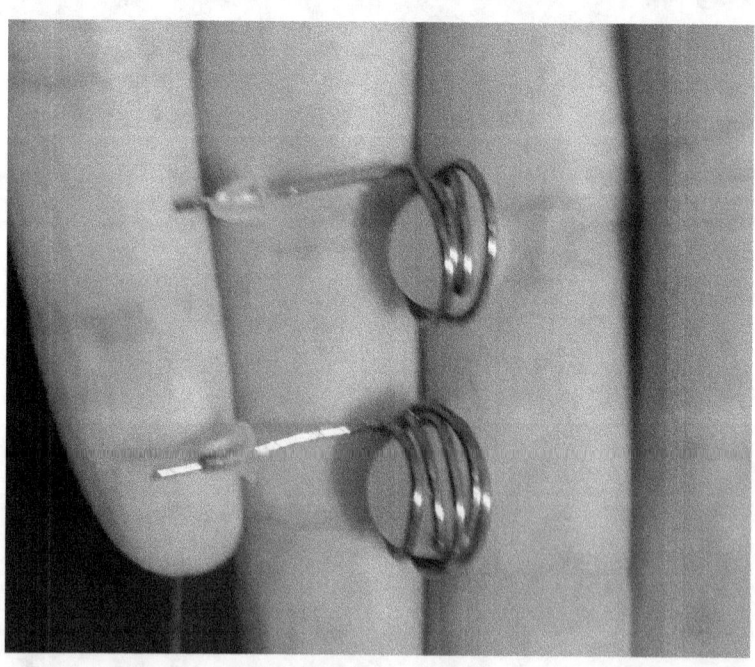

Wire Rose Ring

This is a perfect project for a beginner.

This project is very forgiving as mistakes seem only to make it look better, plus you need very few tools and materials.

Materials and tools needed to make the rose ring are as follows:

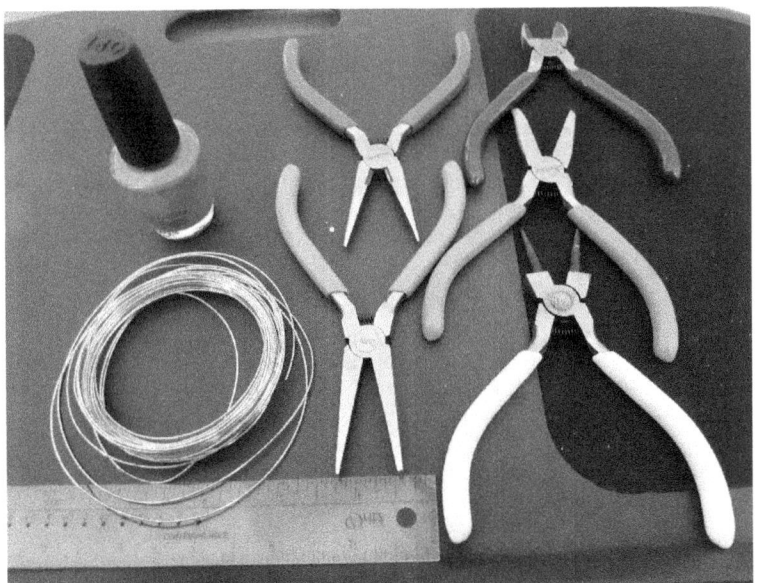

- wire jewelry tools as we previously discussed
- a cylindrical object (a nail polish bottle works perfectly)

- medium gauge wire, 10 inches per rose
- ruler

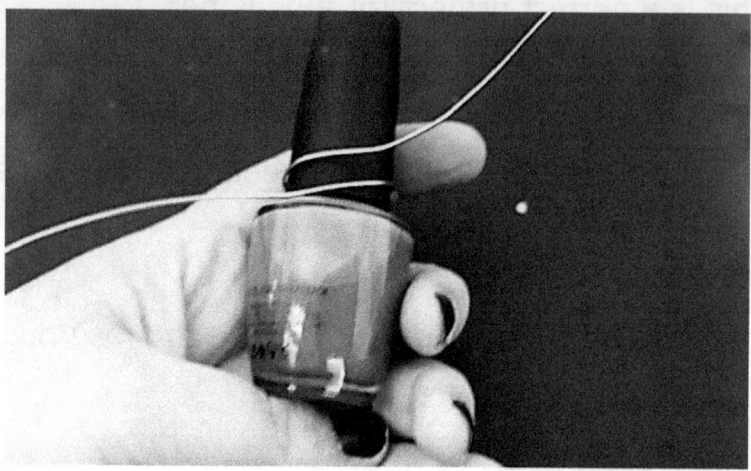

Step 1: Take your 10-inch wire and wrap it around the cylinder so that it is at your halfway point. Create the same length of tails on both sides.

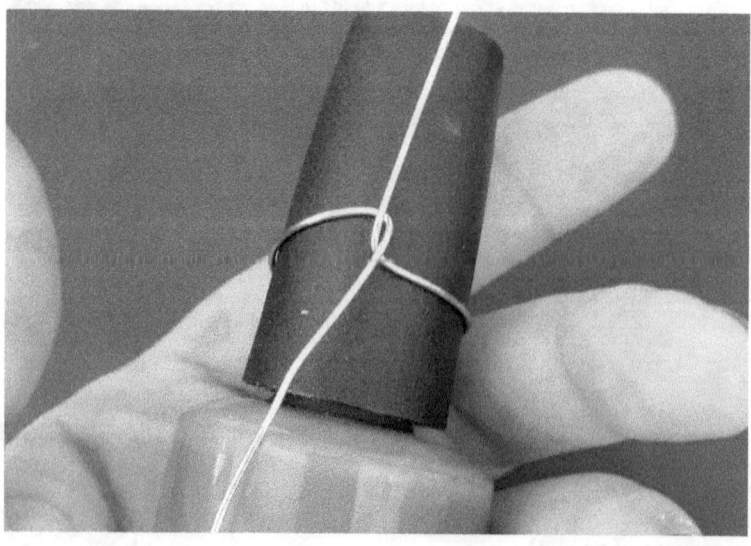

Step 2: Twist one of the wires up 90 degrees and the other down 90 degrees. Make sure to lock the two pieces. Ensure it isn't too loose on your cylinder. You want to make a fairly tight loop.

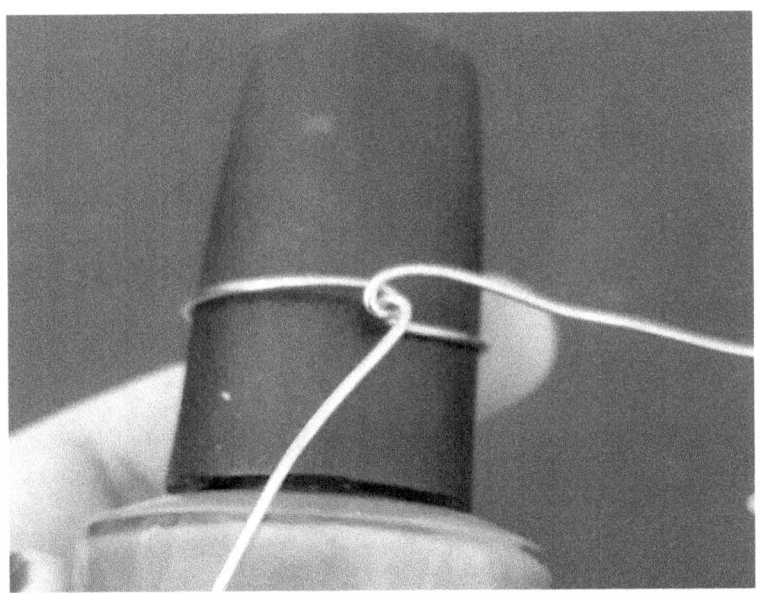

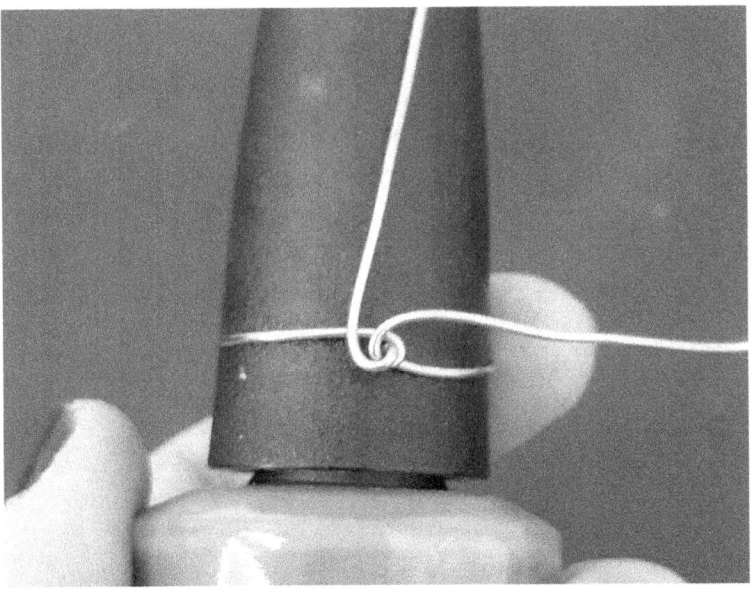

18

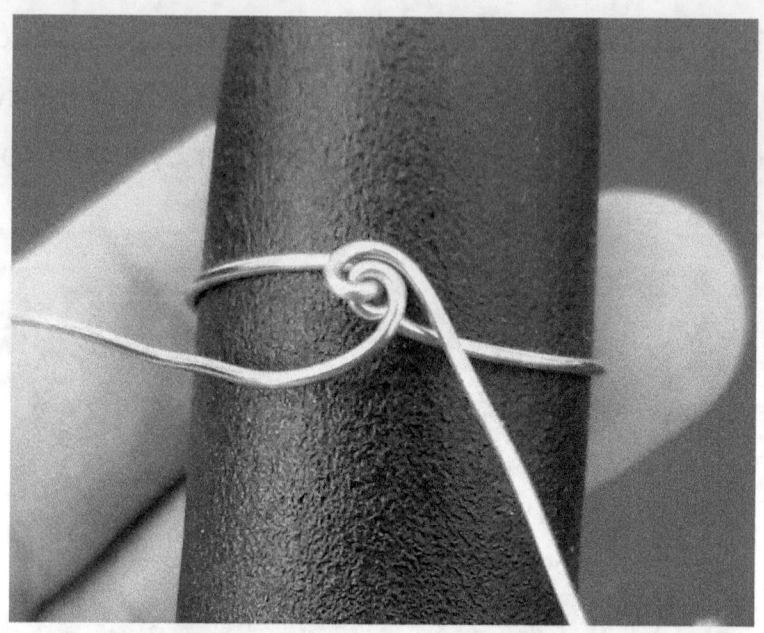

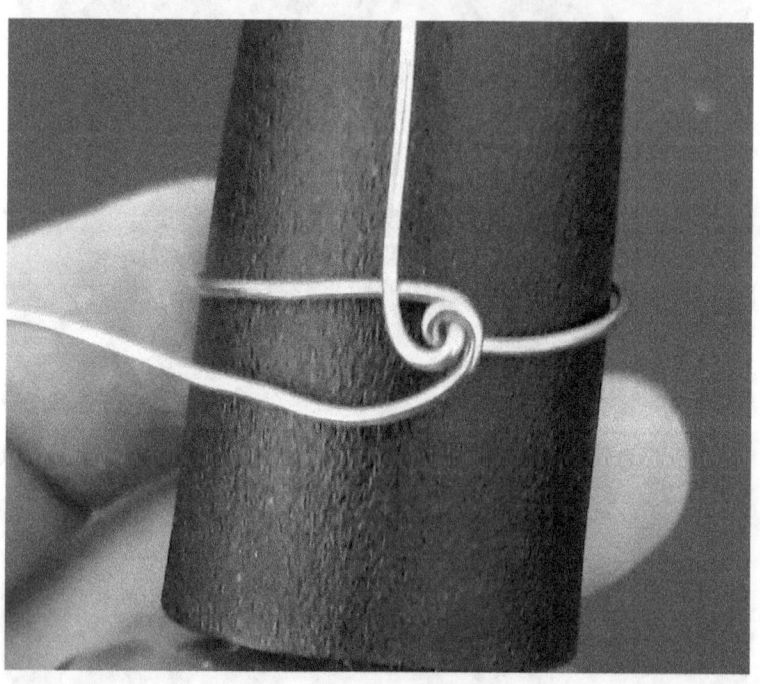

Step 3: Now, you are going to move the two ends around that center point clockwise.

Start by moving one wire 90 degrees clockwise, then move the other around making sure to never cross them over each other.

Move one partially around, then move the other one around as if they are chasing one another.

Step 4: Continue this until you have about 2 to 3 inches of wire left.

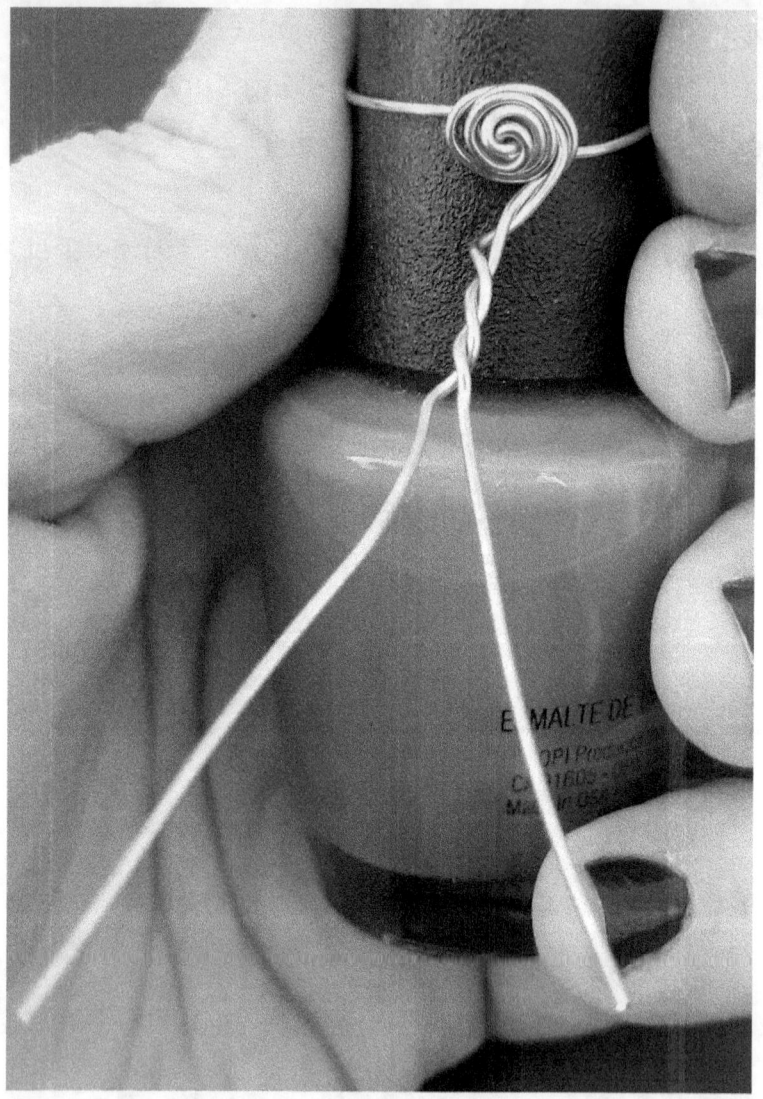

Step 5: Now twist the two strands together a few times.

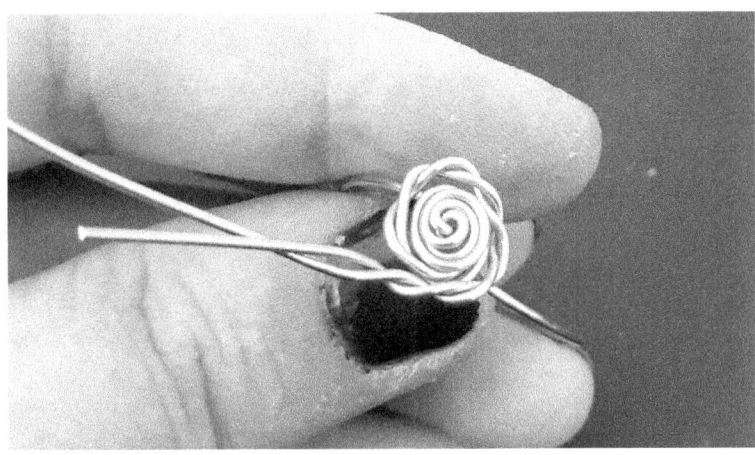

Step 6: Take the piece off the cylinder. Use the twisted strands to continue to wrap around the center you have created. Continue twisting and twirling until you reach the end of the wire or you like the way the rose looks.

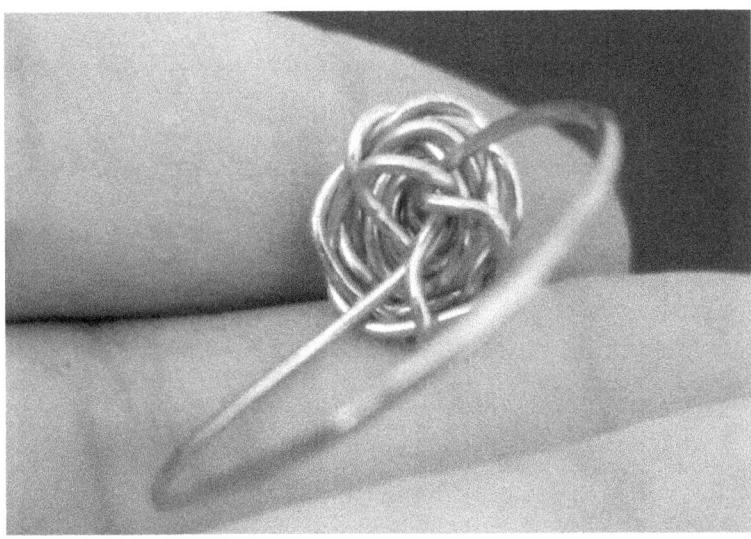

Step 7: Take the ends and bend the sharp points in. Tuck them behind the rose in the wires on the back.

Not only have you made the rose ring, but you have also made the basic rose pattern that we will also use to make the pendant and earrings.

Wire Rose Pendant

This is a gorgeous pendant that begins with the wire rose ring pattern and then easily transforms into something much more in seconds.

The only tool and material you will need are a wire rose ring and wire cutters.

24

Step 1: Cut the band of the ring with wire cutters.

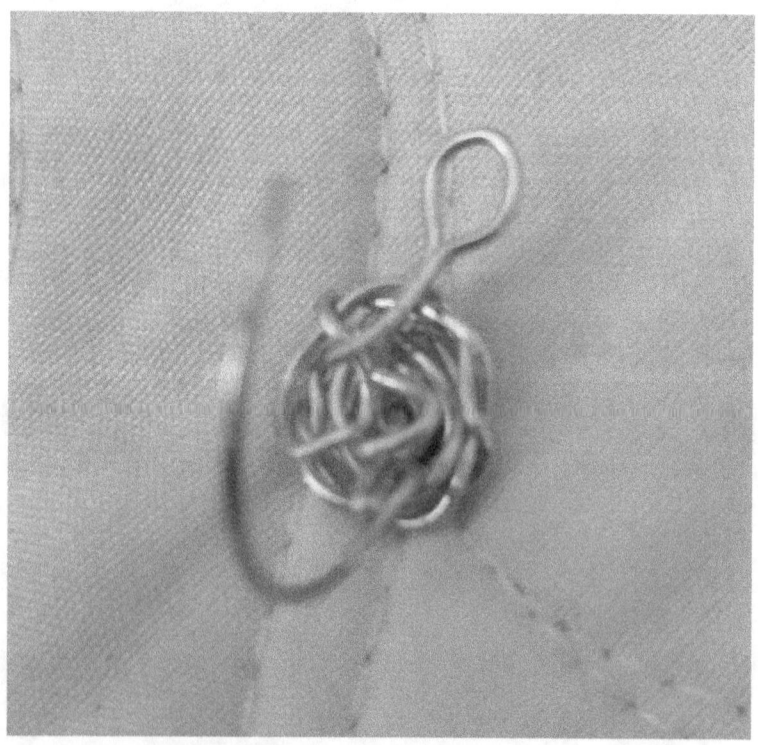

Step 2: Twist one end of the cut wire to make a loop large enough to be able to feed a chain through. Tuck the end into the back of the ring and make sure no sharp pieces are exposed.

Step 3: Cut the other end a little shorter so you can bend it and tuck it behind the rose. Make sure no sharp edges are exposed.

This is what it should look like. This will also be the base to make the rose dangle earrings.

Wire Rose Dangle Earrings

These earrings are created in just a few steps more than the rose ring or rose pendant we have already made.

These are also a great addition to the other pieces we just crafted to make a complete set.

The tools and materials you are going to need are shown below:

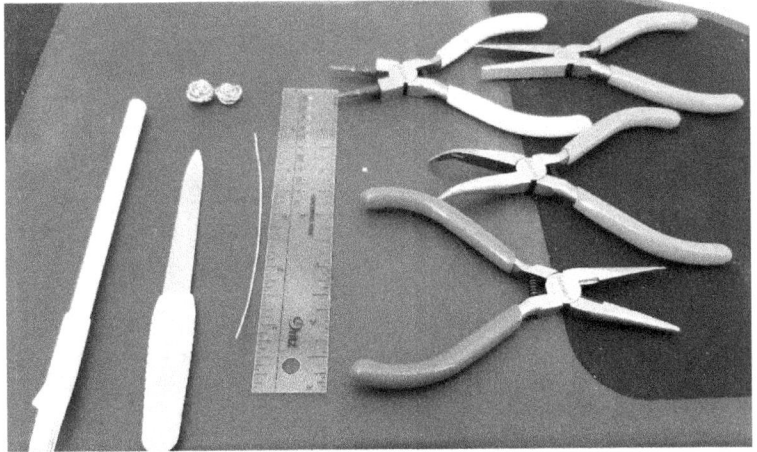

- standard size pencil
- metal file
- 4 inches of wire (it will make 2 hooks)
- standard jewelry making tools

- 2 wire rose pendants similar size and shape

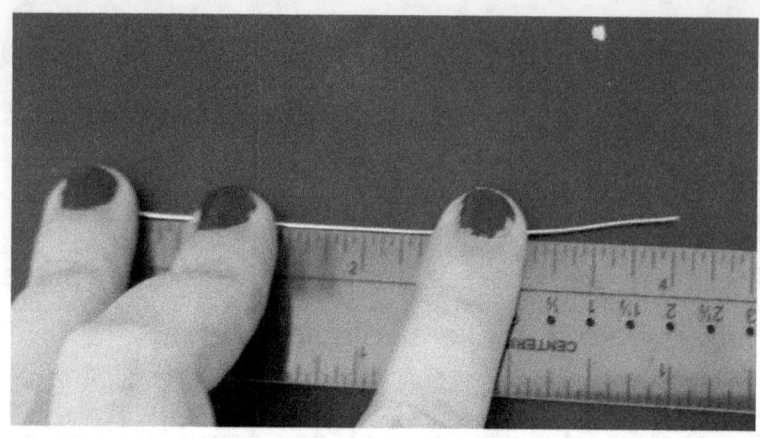

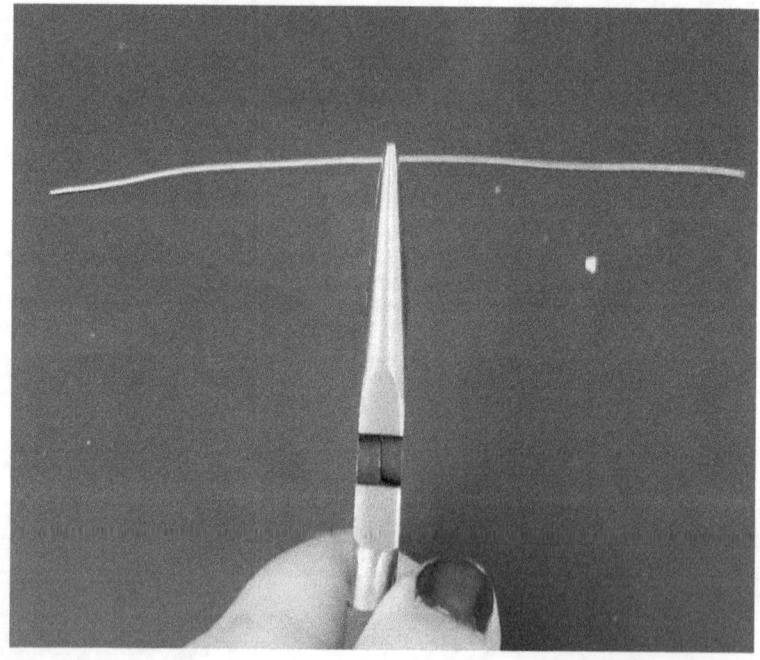

Step 1: Use the ruler to find the exact half (at 2 inches) of the wire (total 4 inches) and grip with needle nose pliers.

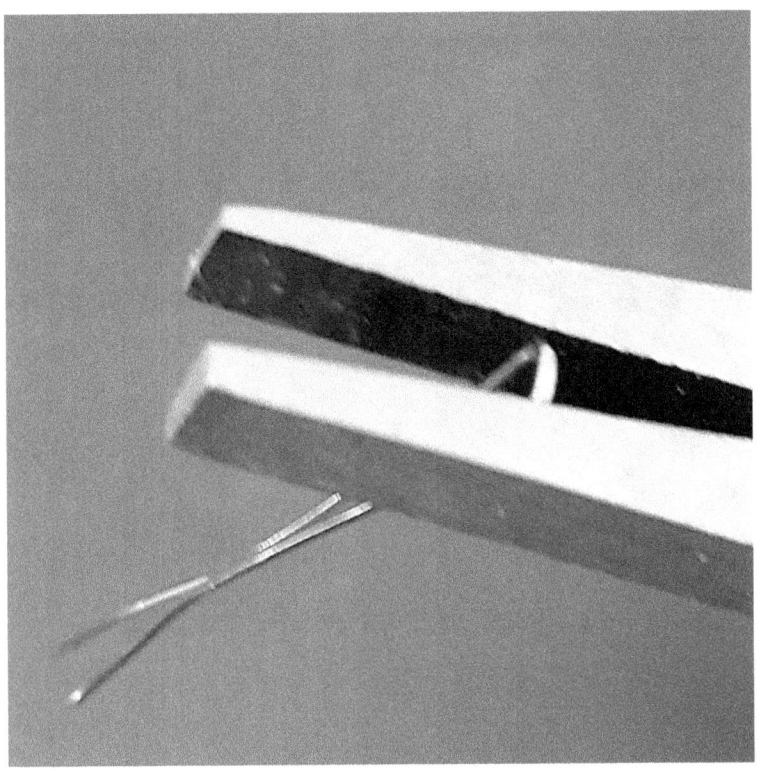

Step 2: Bend the wire in half with the needle nose pliers. Flatten out the fold using the flat nose pliers.

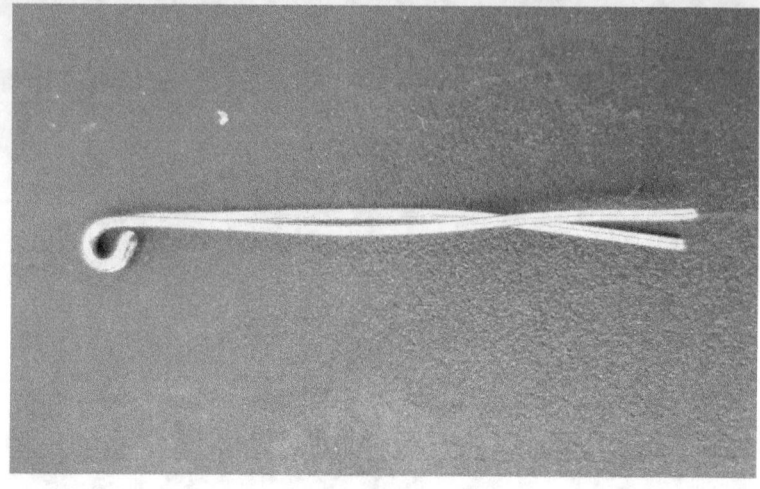

Step 3: Using your round nose pliers, bend the end over in a tight loop with a twisting motion.

This results in a complete loop.

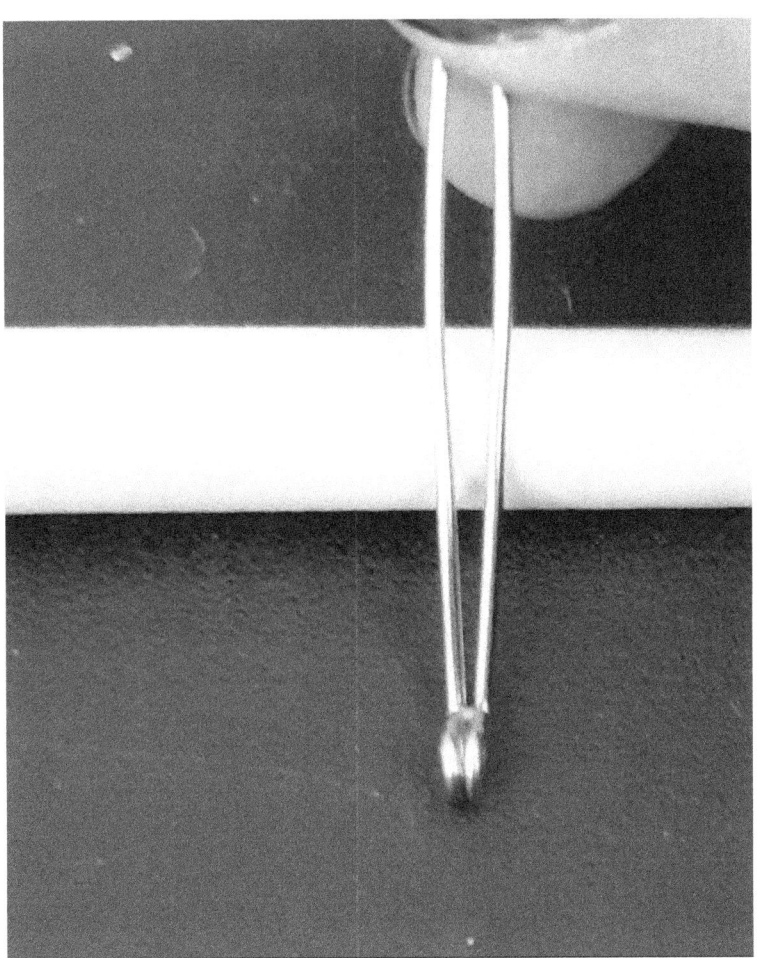

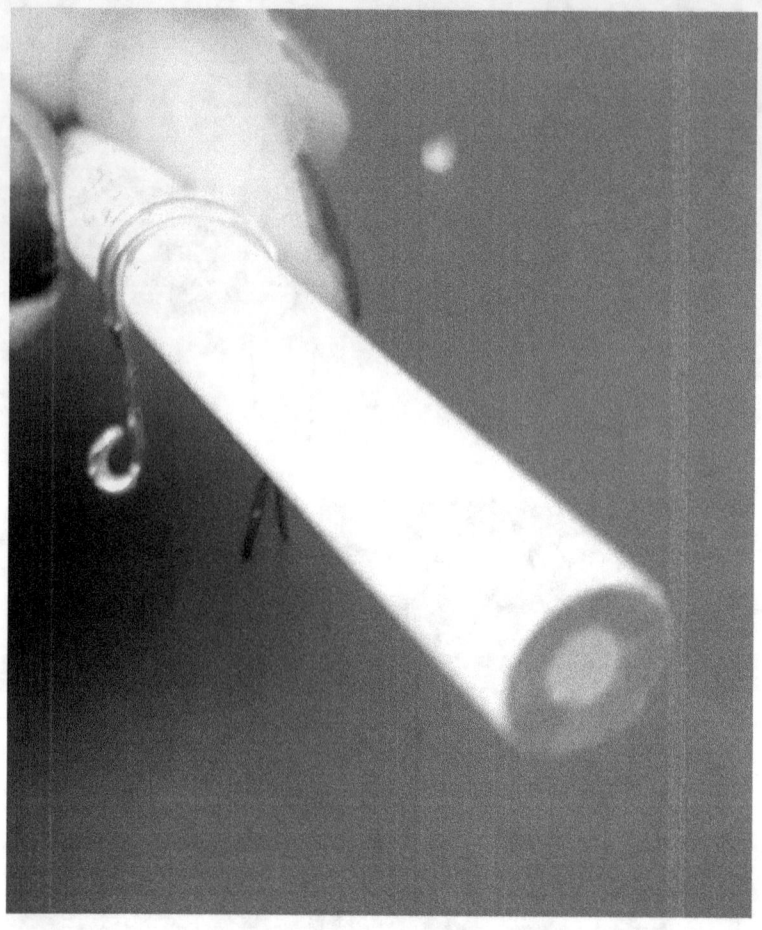

Step 4: Place the pencil behind the piece.

Bend the wires over with your fingers.

Make sure to bend it away from the little loop you just made.

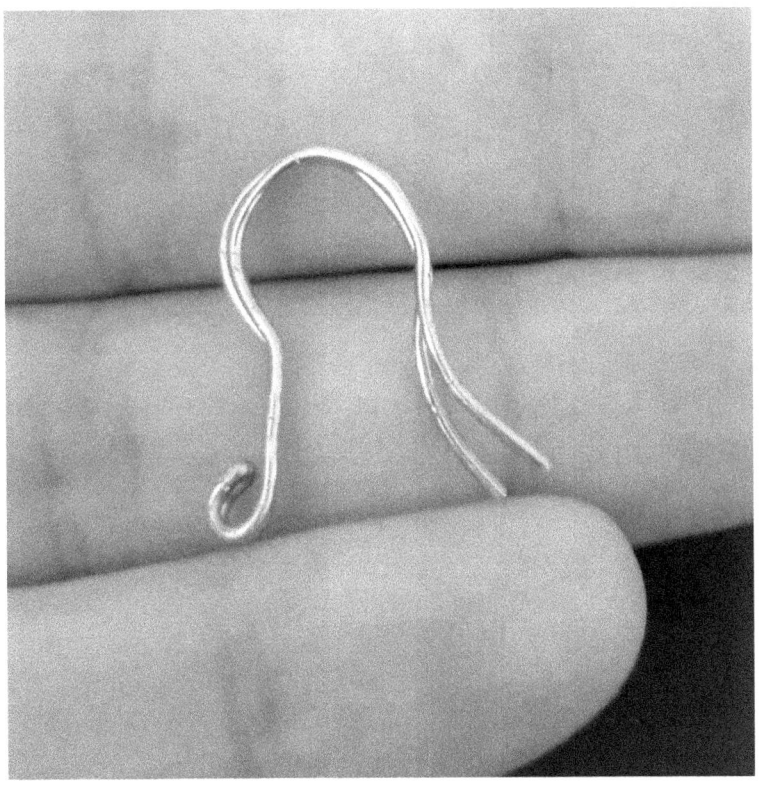

Step 5: Use your pliers to mold the earring hooks the way you want them.

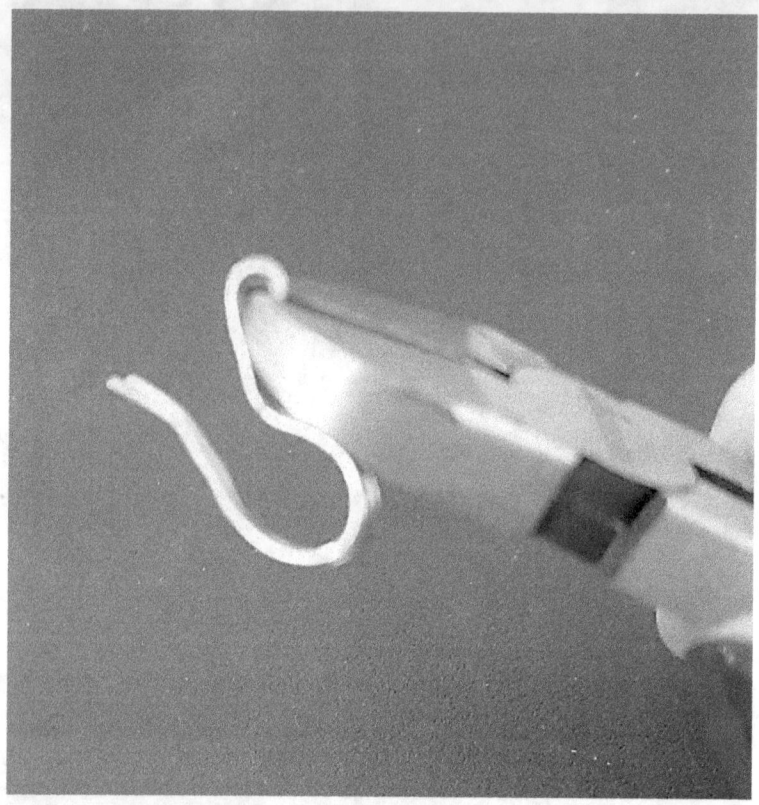

Step 6: Using your wire cutters, snip the bent loop holding the two hooks together.

Note: this is the secret to creating two identical hooks at the same time.

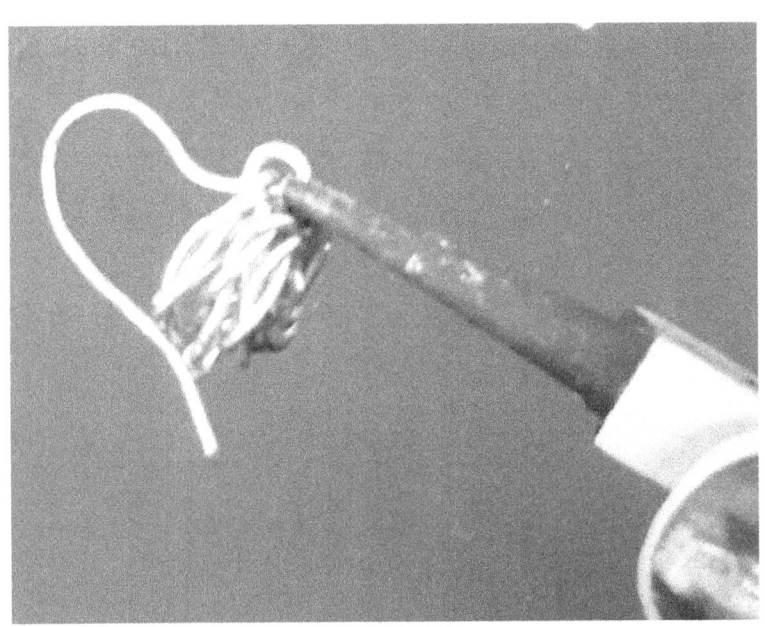

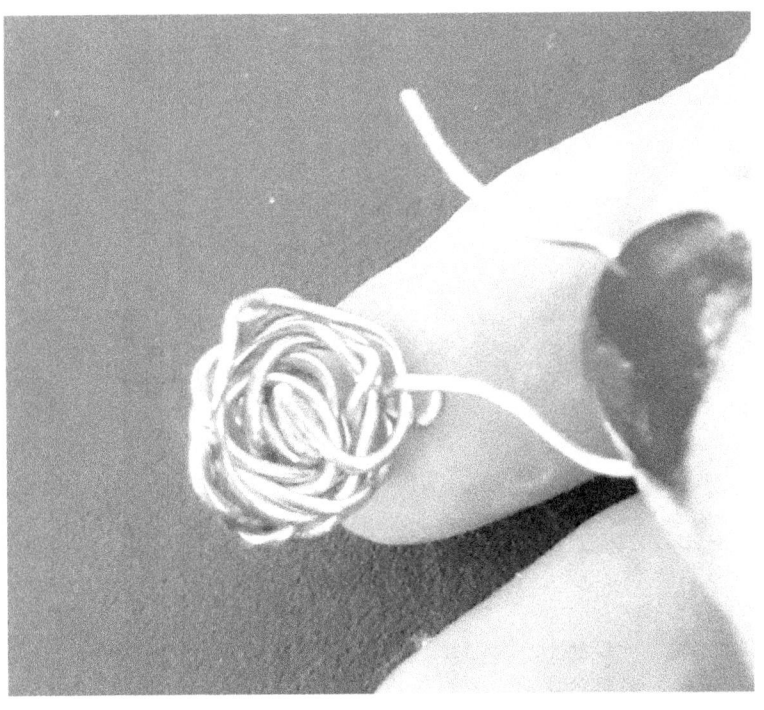

Step 7: Using the little loop opening you just created, hook it on the back of one of the rose pendants. Close the loop making sure there are no exposed sharp bits and the flower hangs well.

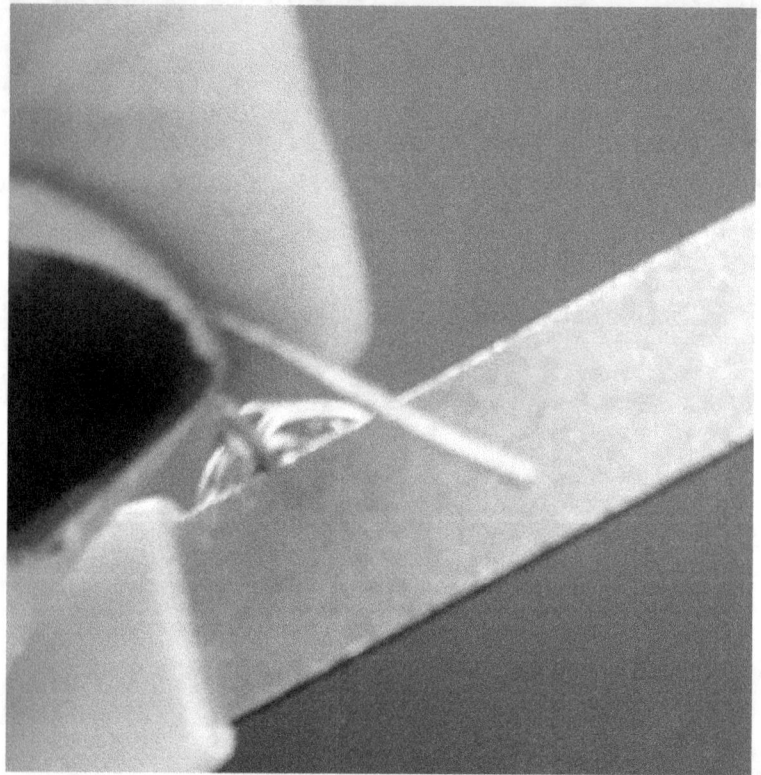

Step 8: Use a metal file on the ends of the wire hooks to smooth the sharp wire.

Remember to only file on the down stroke.

Wire Nest Pendant

This is another project that appears much more difficult than it really is. It is a very stunning pendant that is sure to receive many compliments.

The tools and materials you are going to need for this project are as follows:

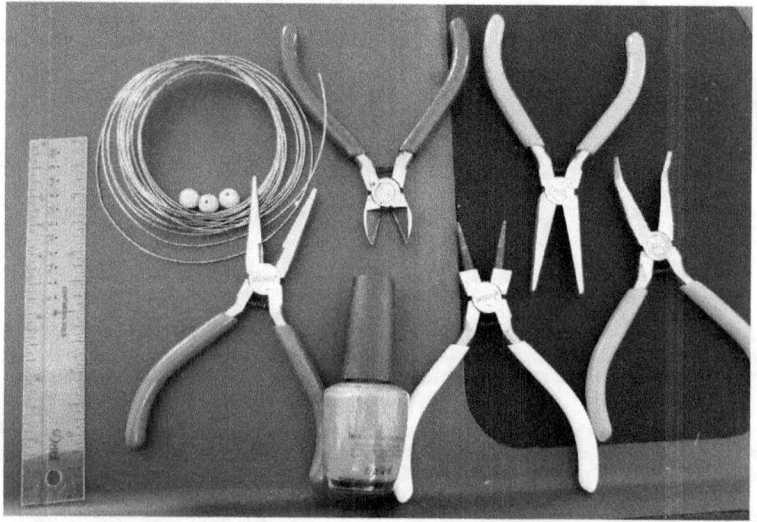

- a ruler
- a cylindrical object (a nail polish bottle works well)
- wire tools
- 2 ½ feet of wire
- 3 beads small enough to all fit into the nest

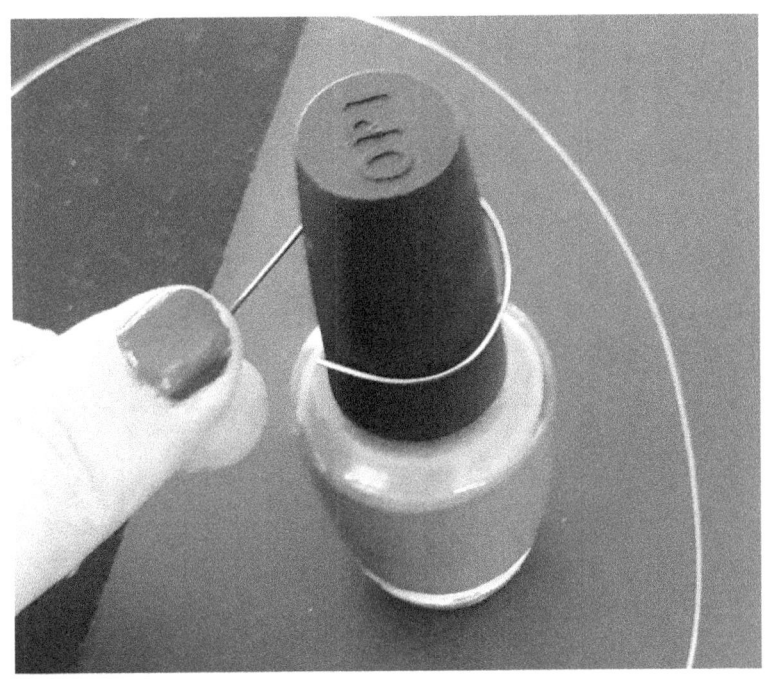

Step 1: First of all, you need to decide approximately how big you want your "nest." The one I made was about the size of a quarter.

Start wrapping the wire around the cylindrical object repeatedly until you get about 4 loops.

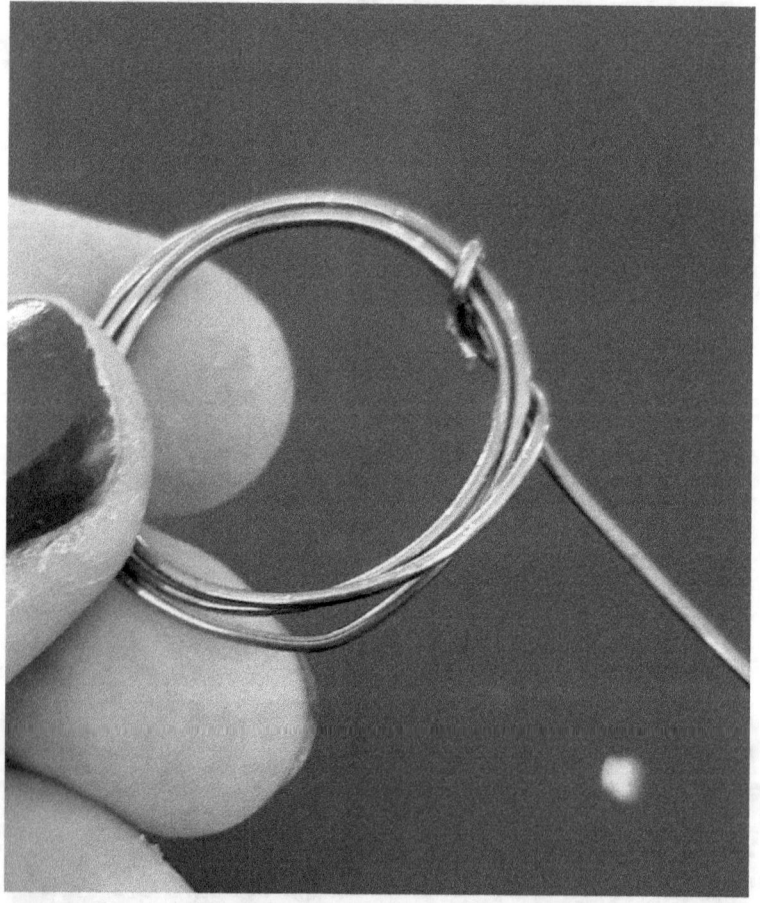

Step 2: Remove the loops from the cylinder. Take the beginning of the end piece of wire and wrap it

around the loops so that there are no sharp wire pieces exposed.

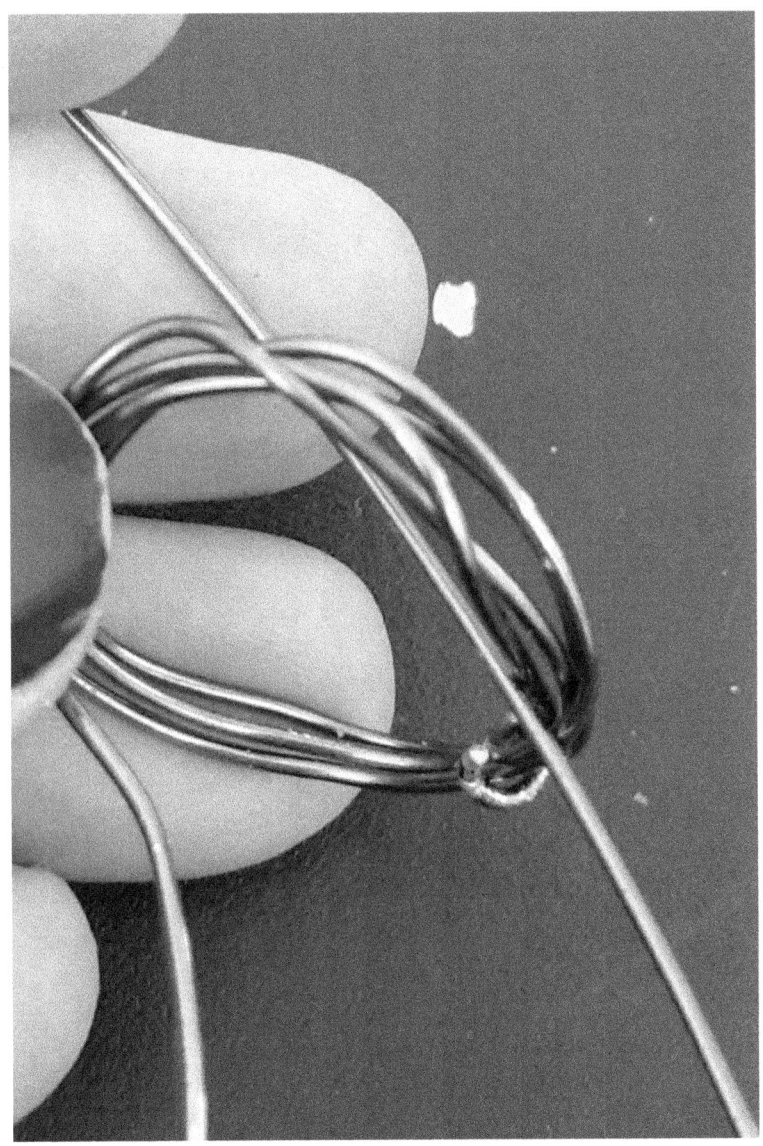

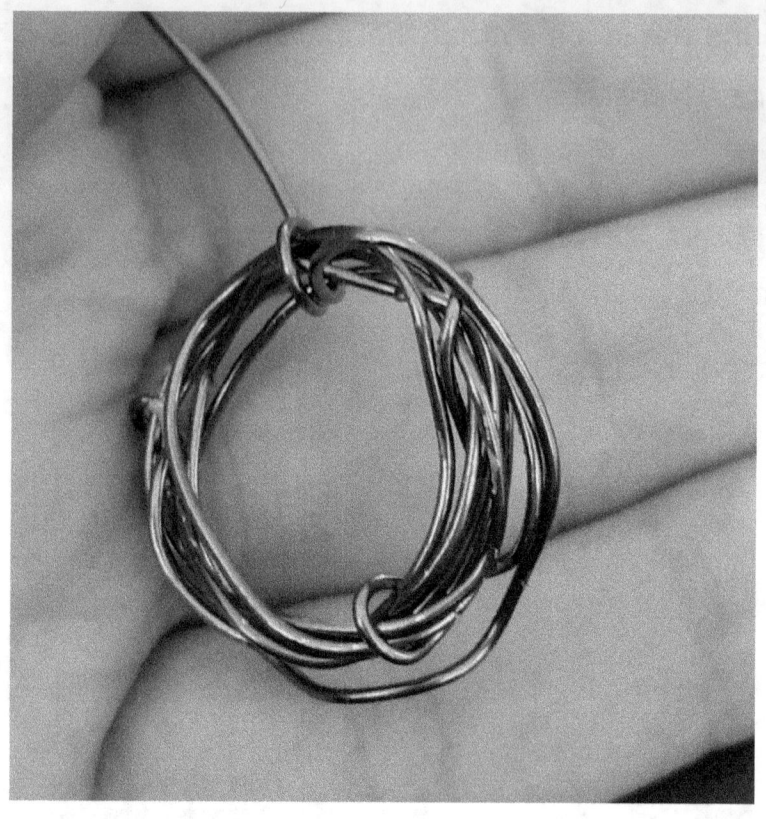

Step 3: Use the long end of the wire to continue bunching and looping the wire round together.

It is important not to make the nest in perfect circles and straight.

Use your tools and fingers to give so a slight bend - make some angled.

Make the loops messy like a real nest.

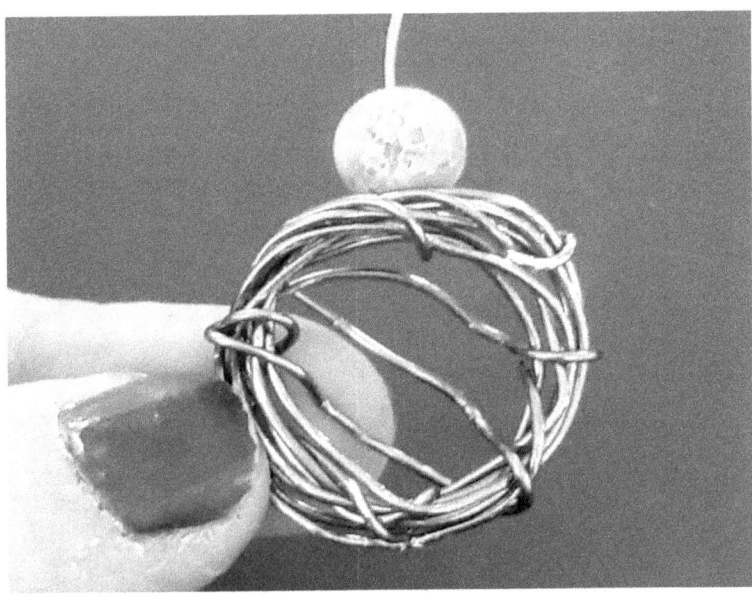

Step 4: When the length of the wire is about 6 inches long or so, and you are happy with the shape of the nest, string a bead on the piece of wire.

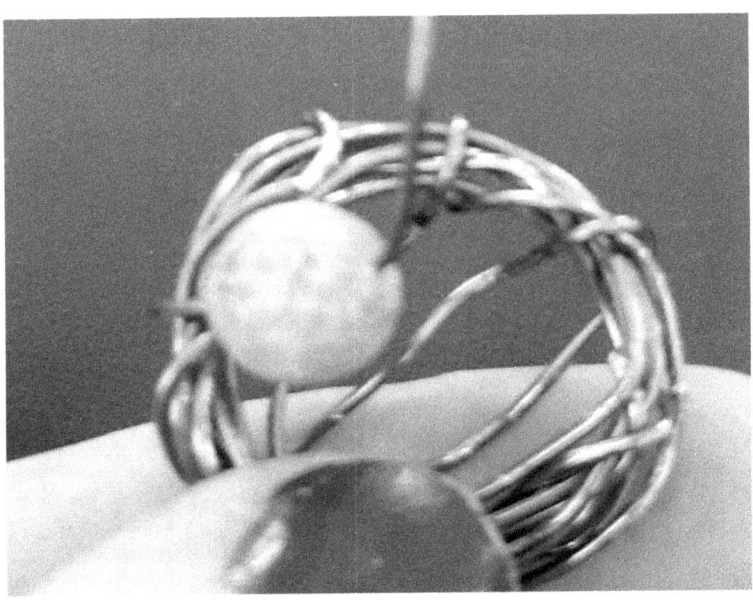

Step 5: Push the bead into the "bowl" area of the nest. Wrap the wire around a piece of wire near the bead to hold it in the nest and keep it secure in its place.

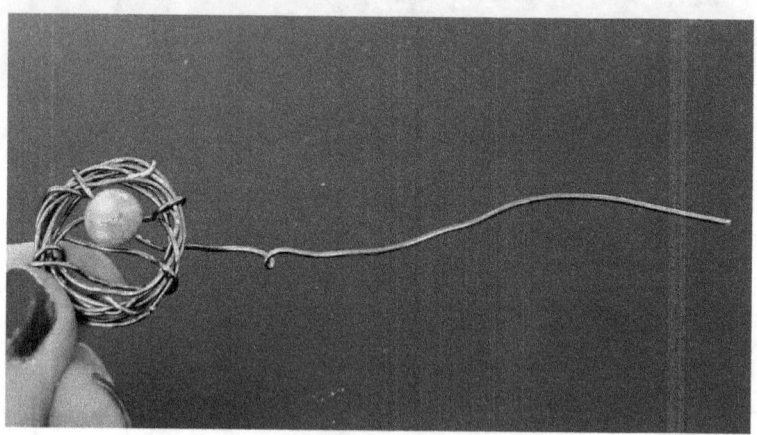

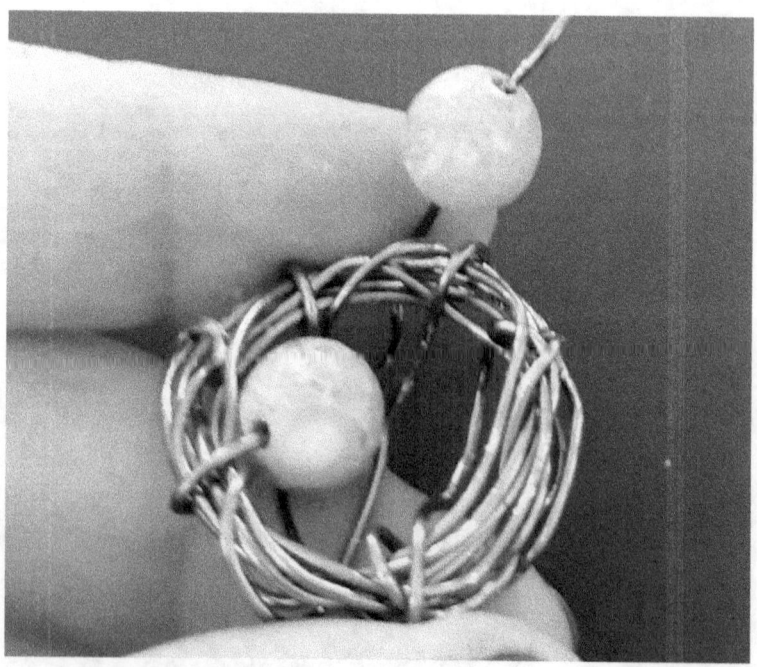

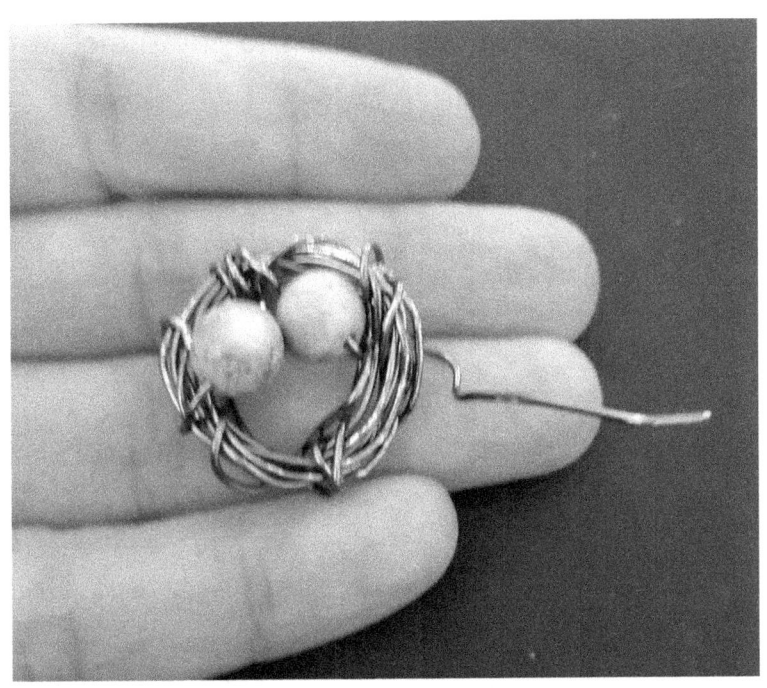

Step 6: Repeat the same steps to add the second and third beads into the nest.

Each bead can be a different shape or color or any combination of colors.

For instance, for a gift for a mom, you can make each "egg" bead represent one of her children.

Step 7: Use the loose end to make a small loop. This loop is made to put a chain through so your nest can be worn as a pendant.

After the loop is made secure the loose wire, trim any excess wire making sure all loose ends are tucked in and not exposed.

These nest pendants are awesome gifts for the moms in your life. I have given many as gifts. I always personalize it by adding one bead or "egg" for each one of the mom's children.

Bead and Wire Studs

These studs are one of my favorite projects. They look nice with jeans and a t-shirt or a nice dress.

Depending on the stone you choose to craft them with, you can really make them personalized, like adding birthstones. The composition of the metal can change the quality. They are very easy to make.

The tools and materials are shown below:

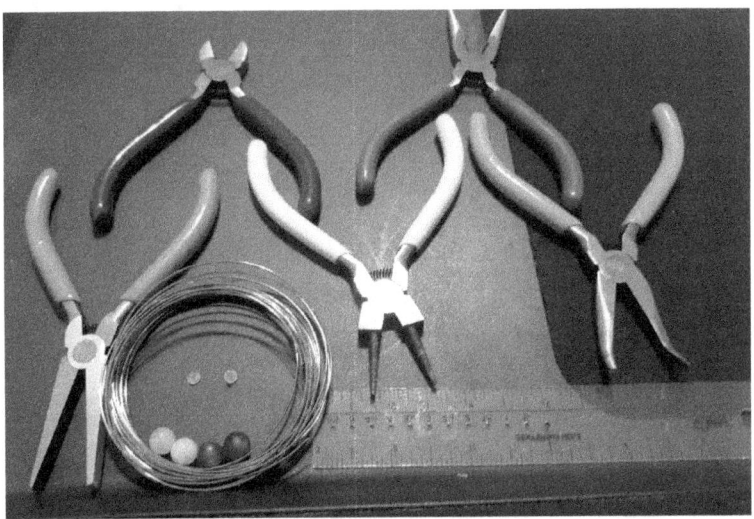

- basic jewelry tools
- 12 inches per pair of jewelry wire of your choice

- ruler
- stones of your choice 2 per pair of earrings
- 2 earring backs per pair
- a metal file (not pictured)

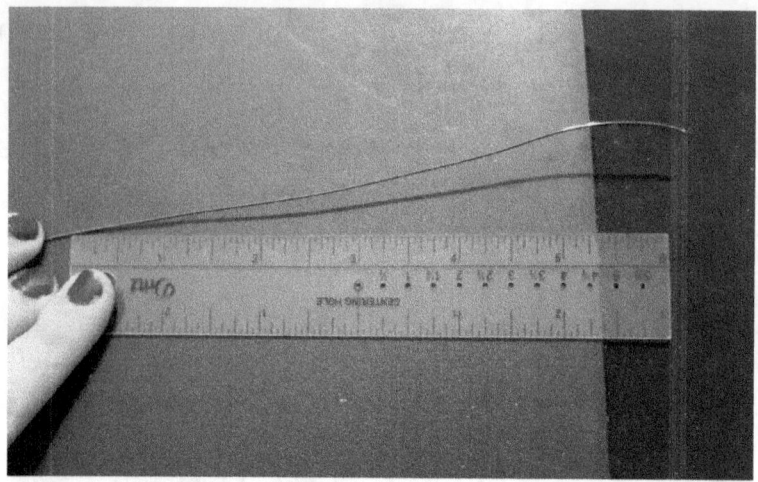

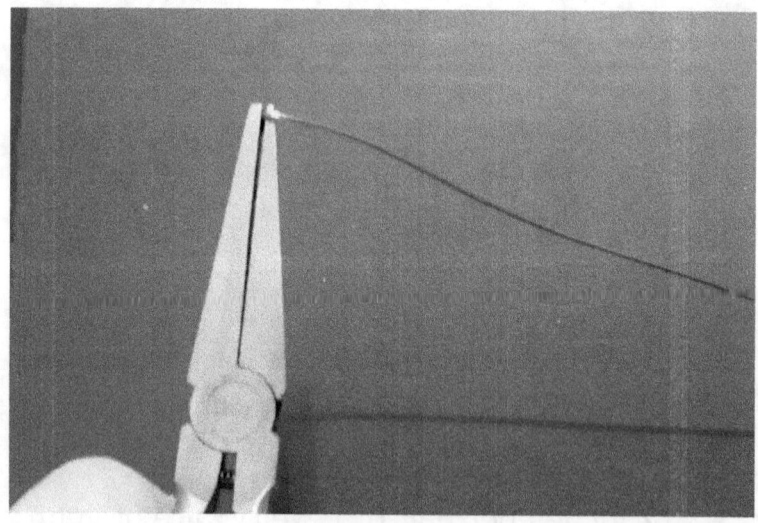

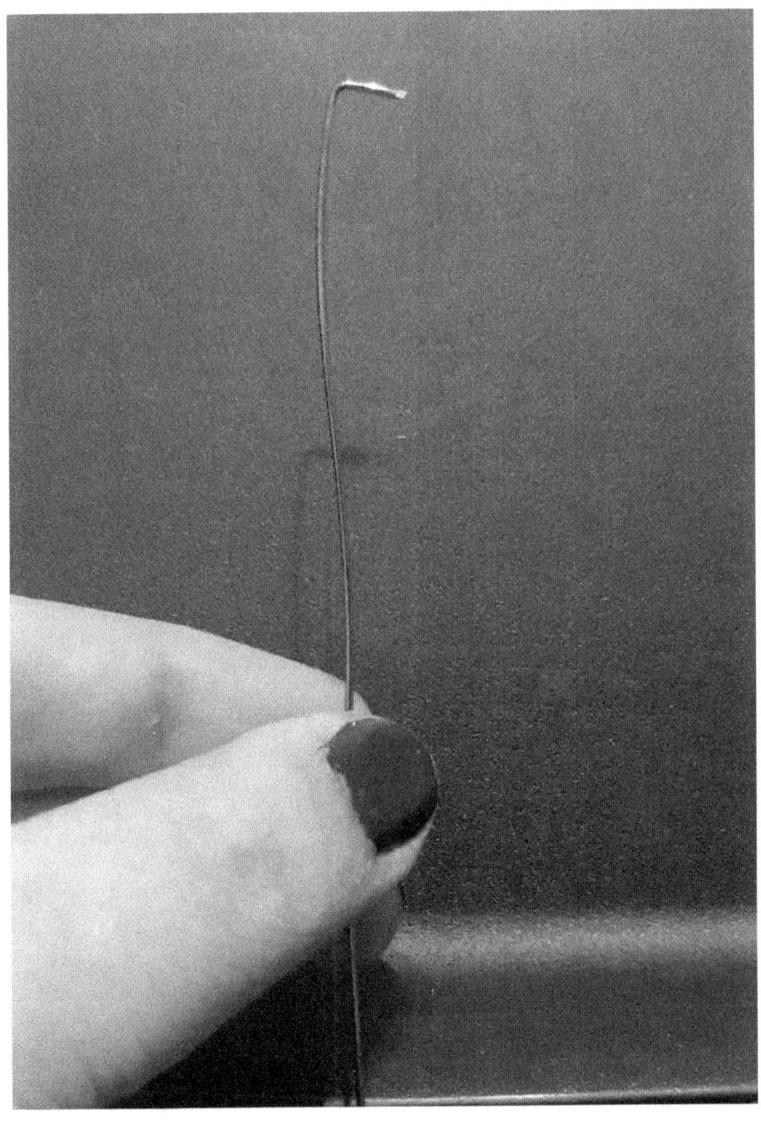

Step 1: Measure and cut off 6 inches of wire. Using your flat nose pliers, bend the tip of the wire 90 degrees.

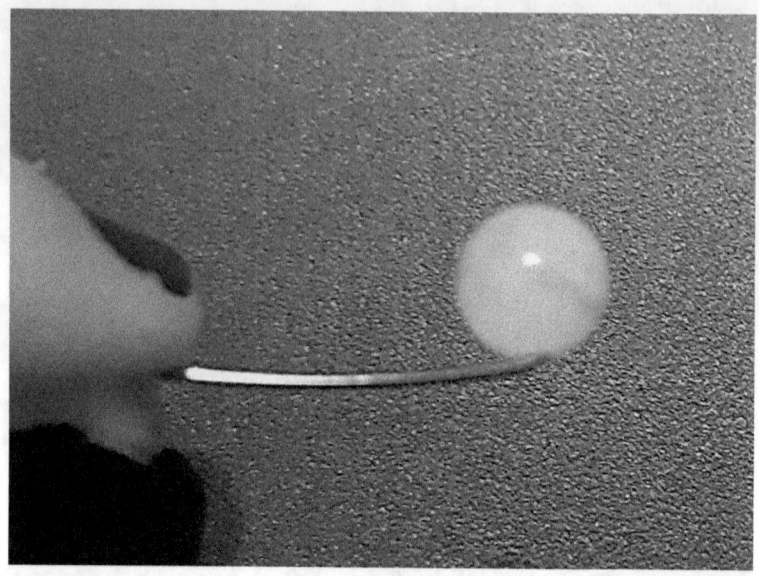

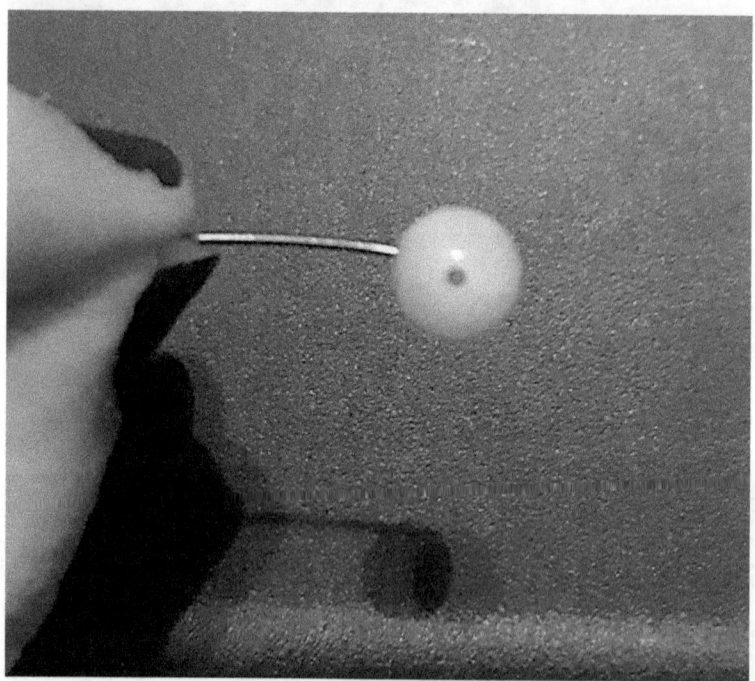

Step 2: Feed your bead onto that little bent end. Make sure that the wire does not come out the other

side of the bead but that the bead sits steadily on the wire.

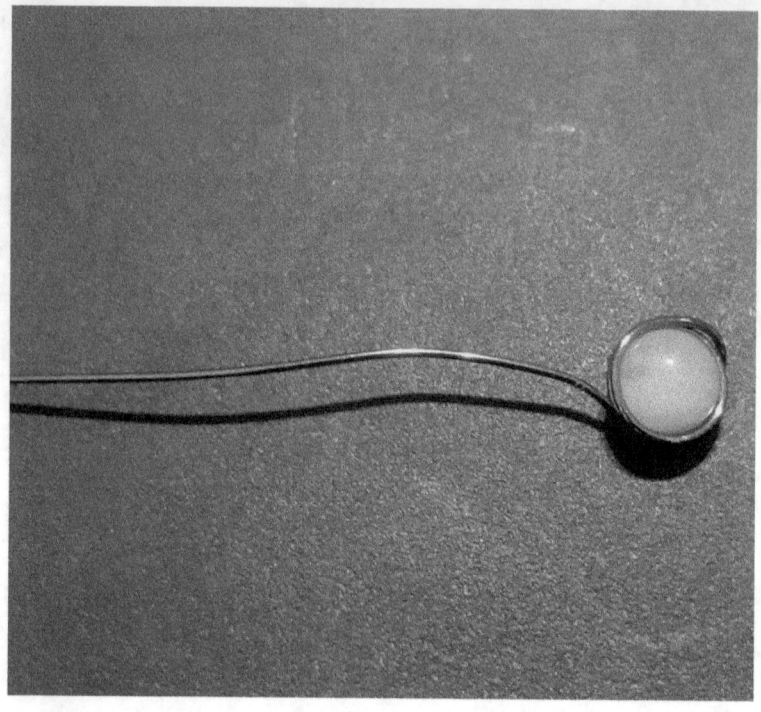

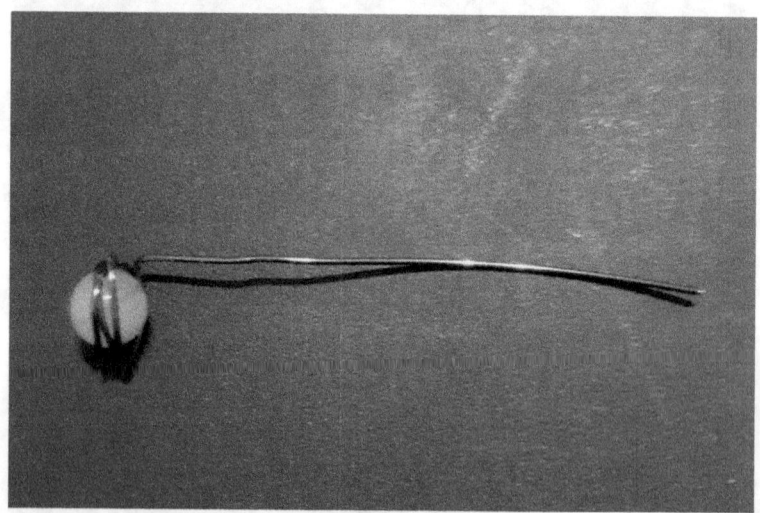

Step 3: Using your fingers or gently using your pliers, wrap the wire around the bead.

55

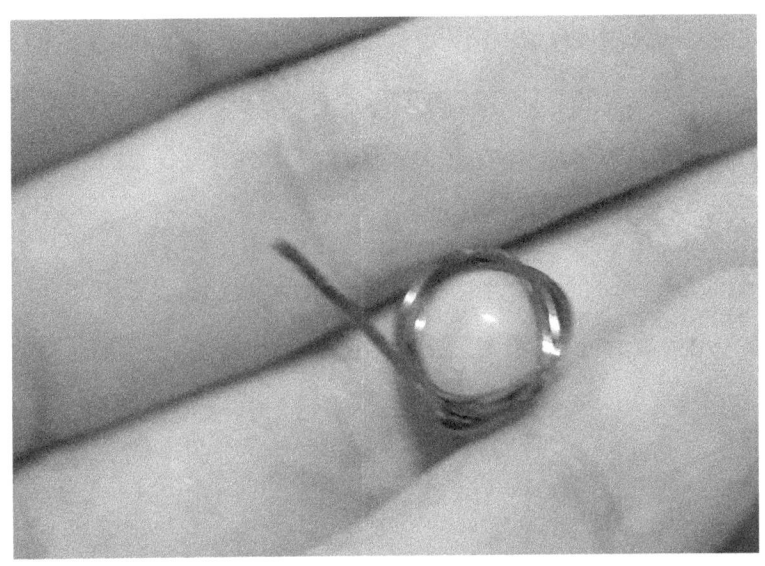

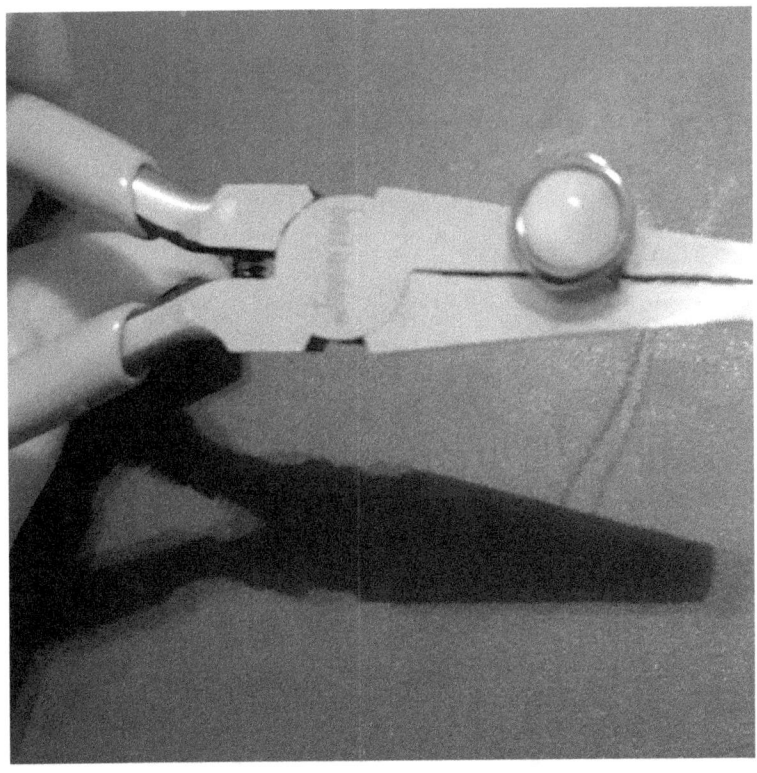

Step 4: When you like the look of the wrapping, or you get to about the length of the tail shown in the picture above, use your flat nose pliers to bend the wire to 90 degrees creating a wire back of the earring.

Trim the back to the desired length and file the back with a metal file. Put the earring backs on them.

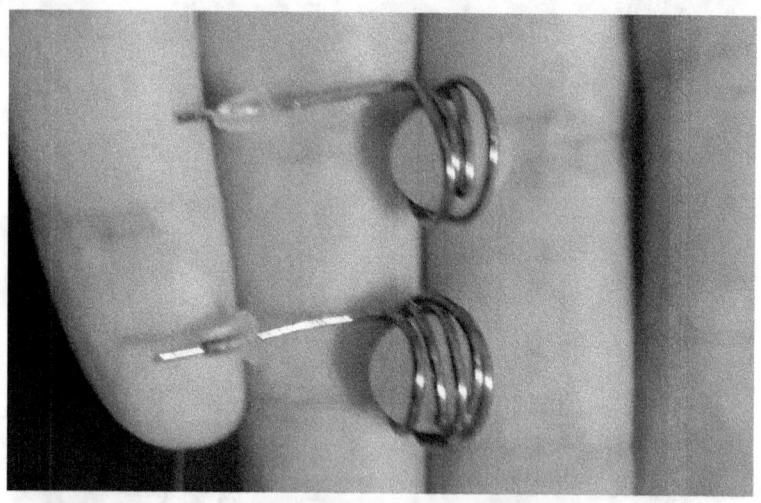

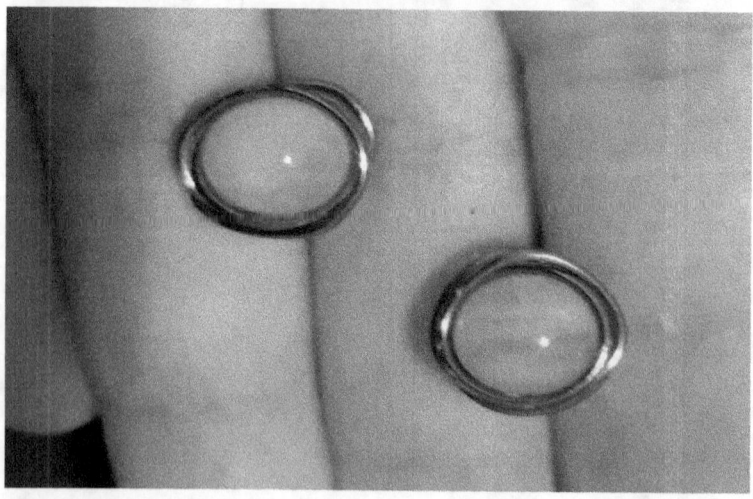

Part 2: Beaded Jewelry

Beaded jewelry is one of the easiest, popular, and most customizable jewelry out there. When looking at options, the choices are endless for beads in size, color, shape, and finish.

There are so many different combinations and choices of beads that it can be difficult to narrow them down for your specific projects. There are also projects that are great for using just a few extra beads.

Having the right supplies and being comfortable with them is really the key to beaded jewelry.

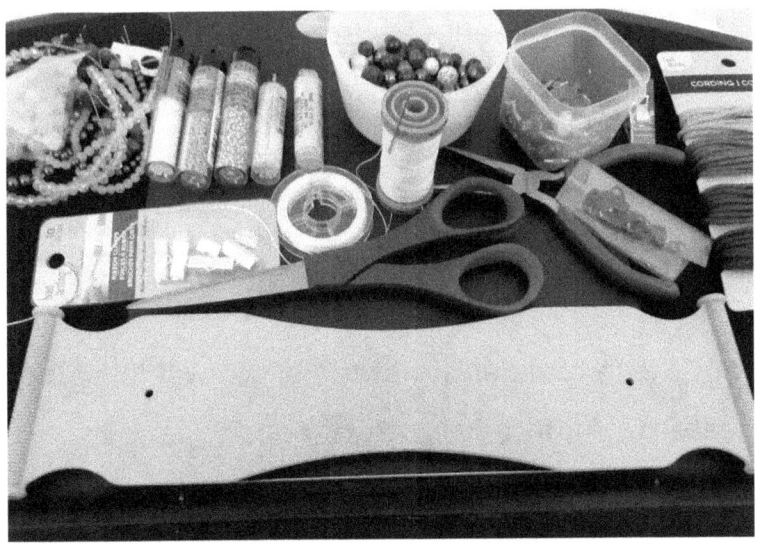

The supplies for all of the beaded projects we will complete are pictured above.

Listed from left to right:

- loose beads in varying colors, styles, and sizes
- ribbon clamps in various widths
- 5 tubes of colored seed beads in an 11/0 size
- beading cord that is stretchy
- sharp scissors
- a beading loom
- small containers to hold loose beads, charms, odds and ends
- thick, strong thread (pictured in a cream color, but darker colors will come in handy)
- long thin needle for beading
- needle nose pliers
- jump rings
- clothespin or binder clip
- leather cording

From these tools and materials, we will learn how to create two different types of beaded jewelry.

Stackable Separate Beaded Bracelets

These bracelets are very easy to put together and mix and match perfectly.

The materials and tools you will need are as follows:

Listed from left to right:

- strands of jewelry beads
- long thin beading needle
- clothespin or binder clip
- beading cord that is stretchy
- needle nose pliers
- sharp scissors
- a small container for holding loose beads, charms, or decorations

Step 1: Use the stretchy cord to measure around your wrist.

Double that amount and add a few extra inches.

Cut the off the long piece of cord. Thread one end with the long thin beading needle. Tie the two loose ends together. This gives you a double threaded needle tied off with knots on the other end.

Then I clipped the knotted end to the edge of my work surface and began stringing beads down the needle and onto the string

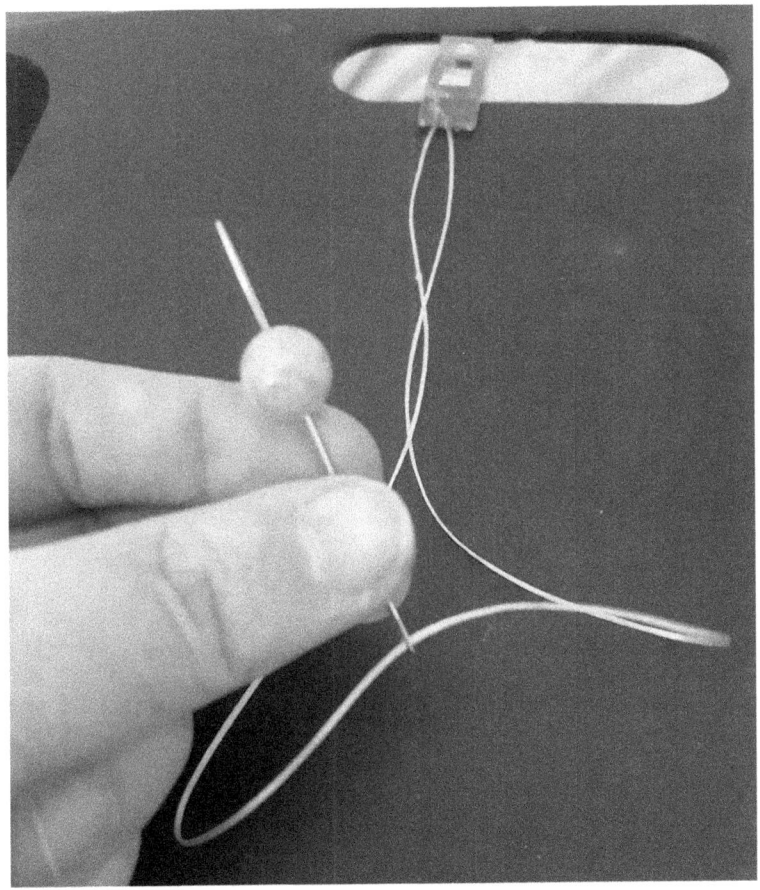

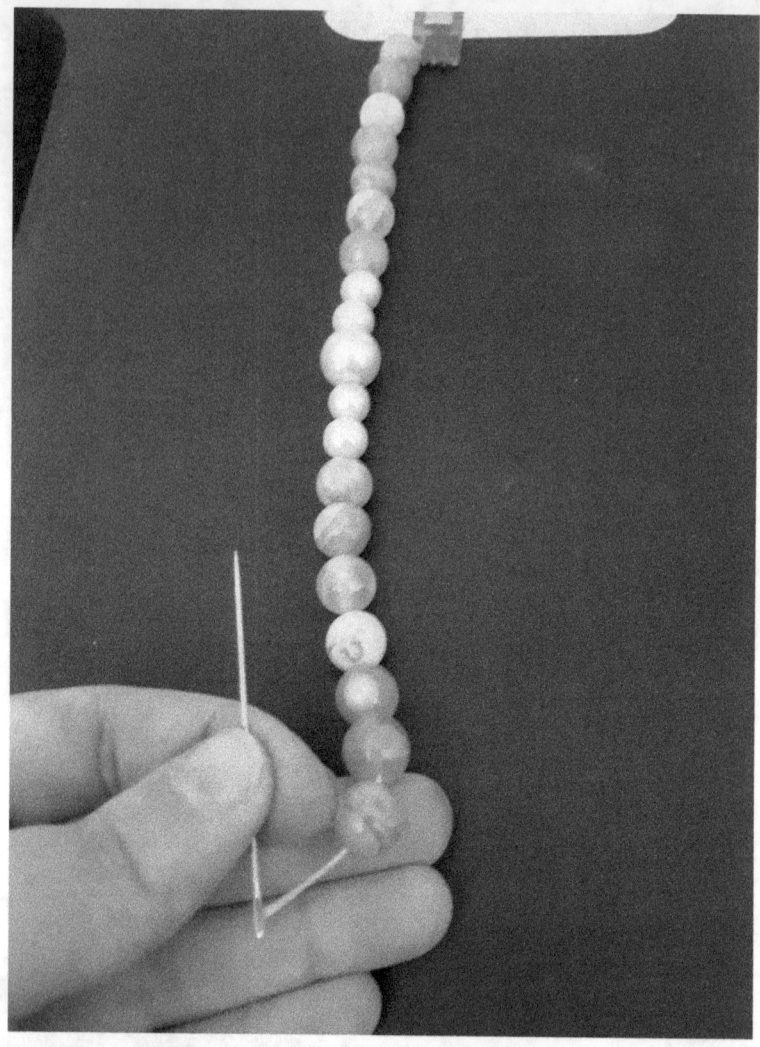

Step 2: Integrate the pearl detail in the strand process continuing until very close to the end of the cord.

Cut off the needle and tightly tie the two ends. In an effort to hide the knots, slide the beads over the knots so that they are covered.

Both of these bracelets were made in the same manner.

67

Step 4: This bracelet has a large charm that I slipped onto the string during the beading process. I then continued stringing around it.

With this variation, I tied my thread to one edge of the charm.

Then I beaded it and tied the other end to the other side of the charm.

These types of bracelets really can be made in any size shape or color and include charms or toggles as well as other decorative items.

Also, they are stackable and can be mixed and matched. Wear as many or as few as you like.

Choose all the same color family or mix up the colors.

Wear only ones with certain types of charms or mix charms and toggles and details.

Beaded Wrap Bracelet

These bracelets are popular right now and can be very expensive. However, they are cheap to make, easy to craft once you get the hang of the beading, and highly customizable.

In order to make a bracelet like this, you are going to need the following items.

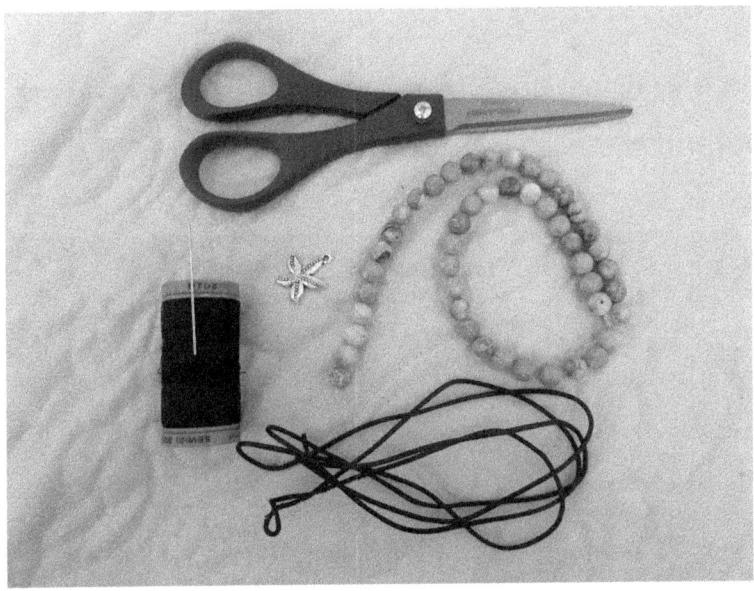

- 15 inches of 6mm beads
- 40 inches of leather cord
- dark, strong, durable thread
- long thin beading needle
- a charm to be the closure
- sharp scissors
- safety pin or binder clip/

Step 1: String your charm on your leather cord. Slide the charm to the middle of the cord and fold the cord in half.

Thread a long length of thread with the beading needle. Use the ends of the thread to tie a knot on the leather cord where it is folded.

Tie a knot as close to the charm as you can with the tread and leather.

Step 2: Using the threaded needle, go over the right cord, through the bead, and over the left cord.

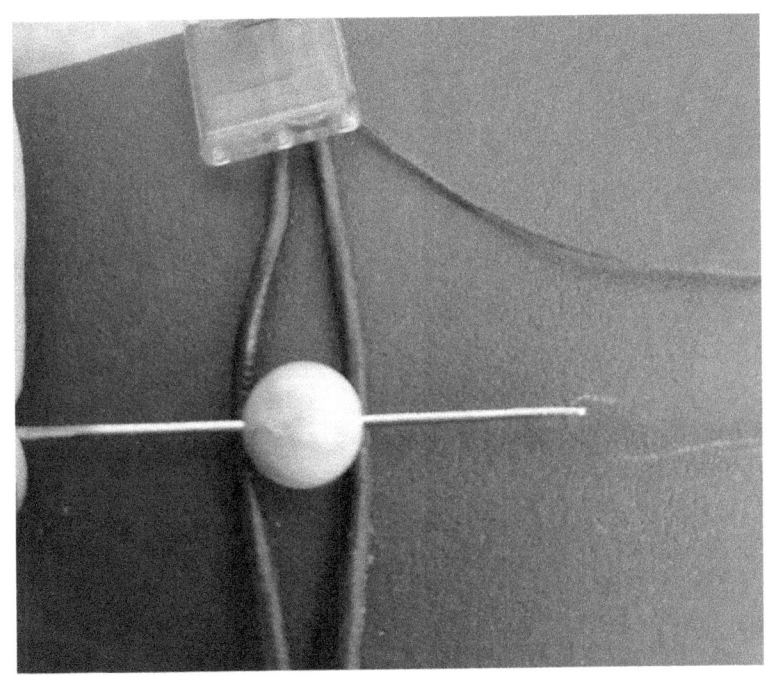

Step 3: Ensuring the bead is in the middle of the two cords, turn your needle around. Go under the left cord, through the bead, and under the right cord.

Pull the needle all the way through until you feel the bead lock into place. The first few beads are always the most difficult to get the cords straight and get the pattern going.

76

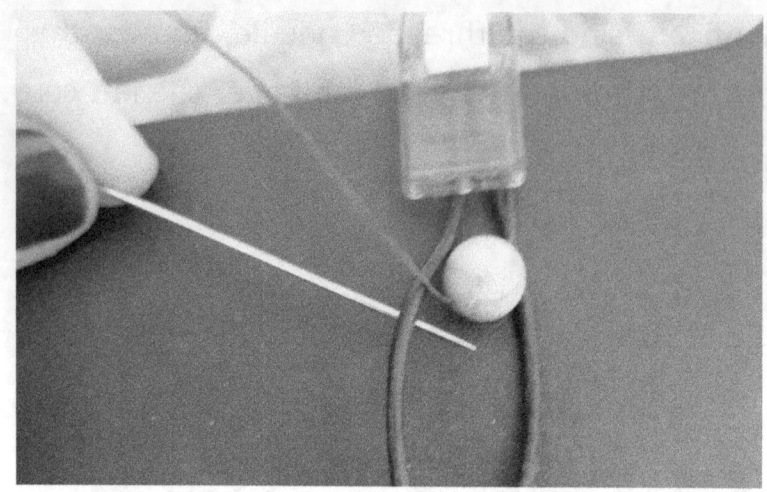

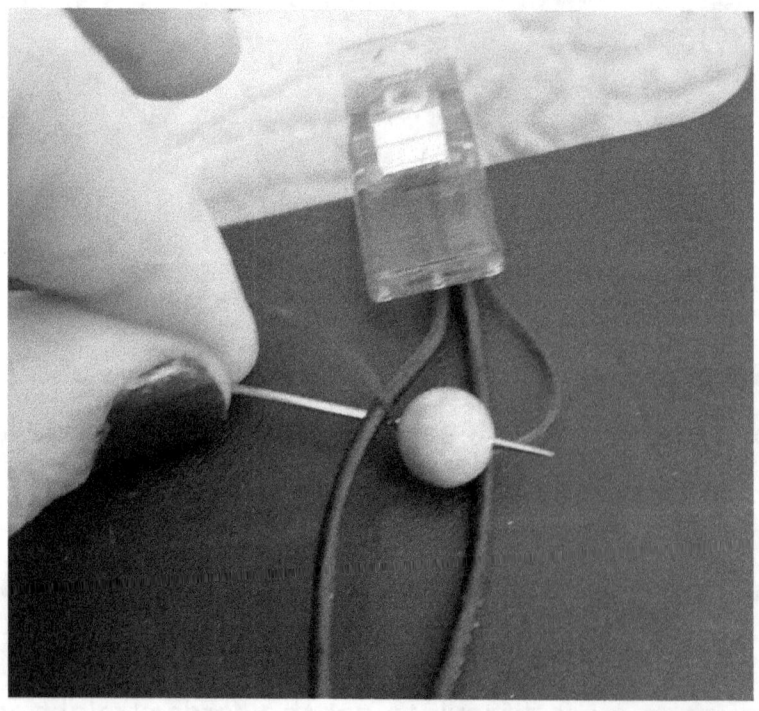

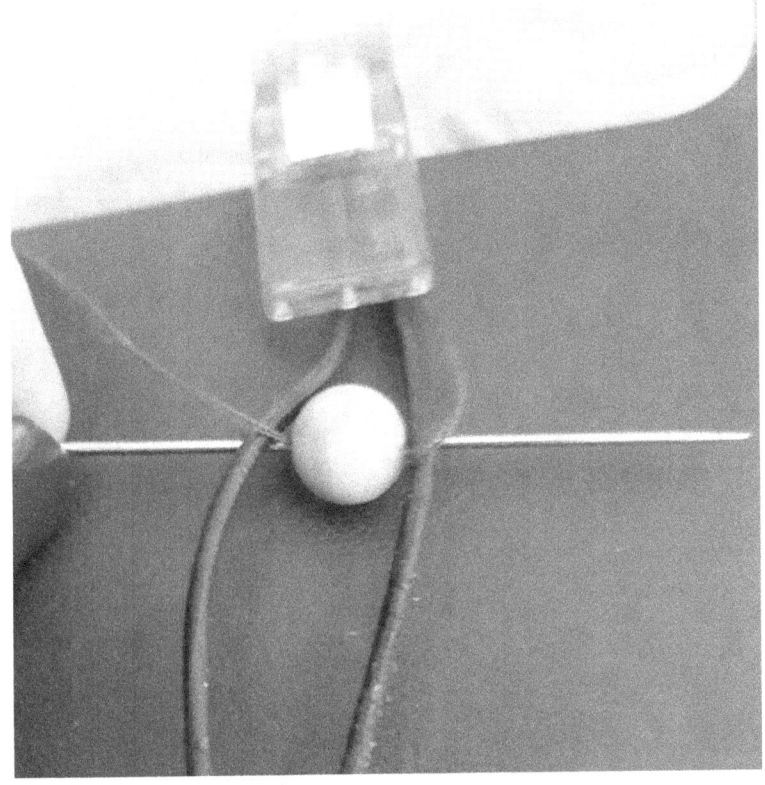

Step 4: Turn your needle around, from the right cord, pick up a new bead, and then go over the left cord.

Turn your needle around and go under through and under - all the way down until the desired length is reached.

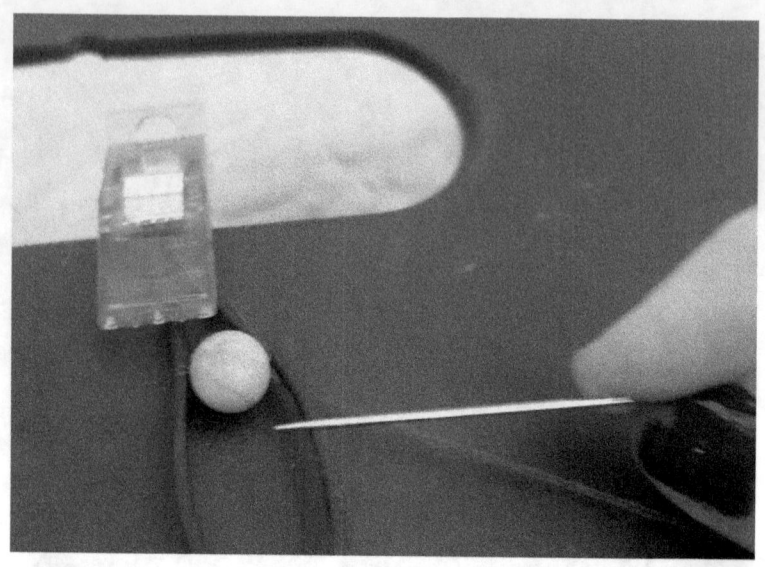
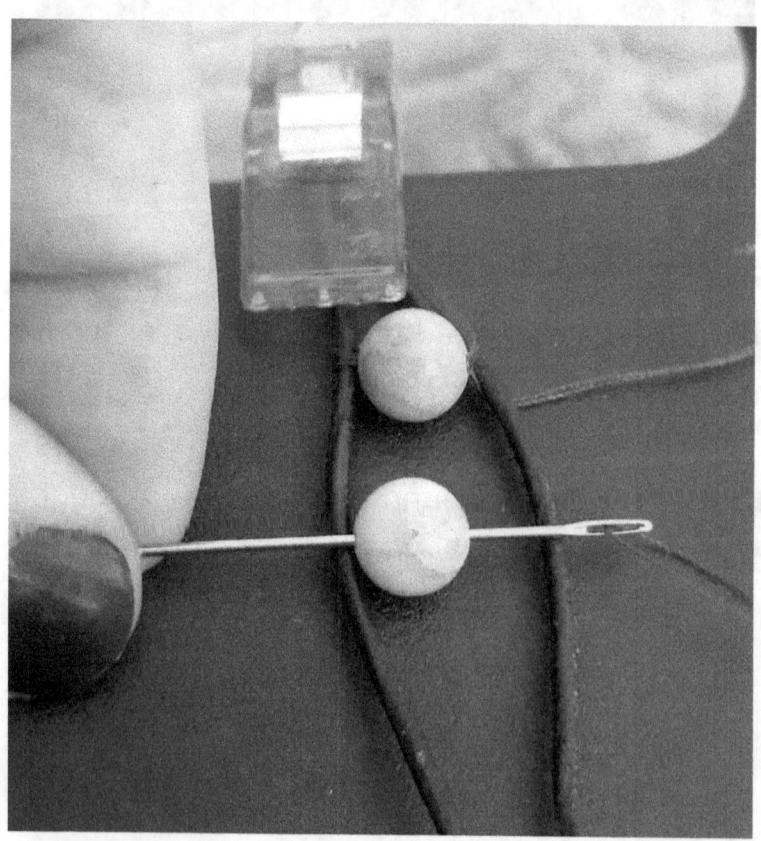

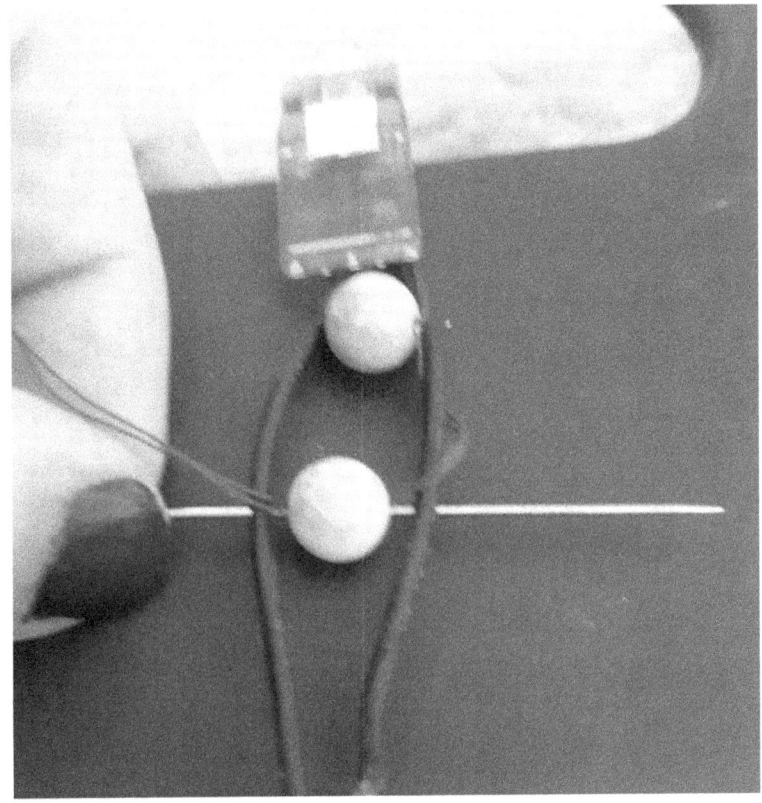

Step 5: Once the desired length is reached, go back up to the bead above the final one.

Reweave your needle through the bead and cords so that the end is secure with no chance of falling apart.

Step 6: With the leather cords and the thread tie a knot.

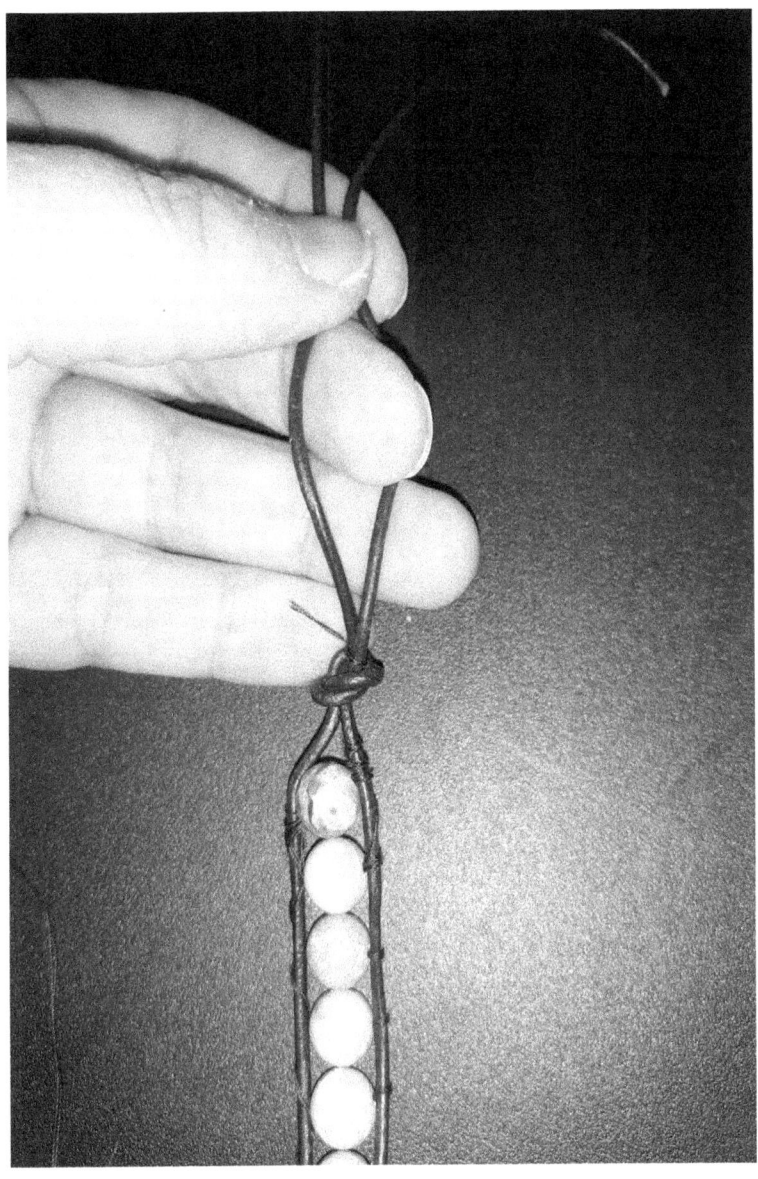

Step 7: Leave a small space between the first knot and the following knots so your charm will fit through.

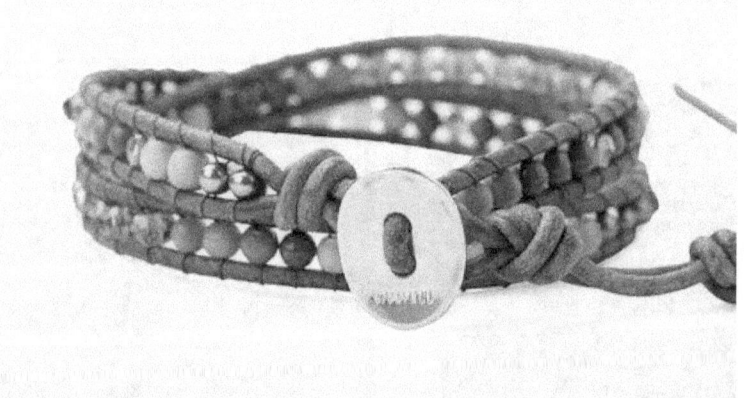

Crafting with a Bead Loom

This is a fun project that can be made simply enough for beginners or advanced and elegant enough for more seasoned crafters.

Working the bead loom is easy to do and results in a piece that is really nice. However, it takes some patience to weave on the loom and work with the miniature seed beads.

The tools and materials are listed below:

- bead loom
- seed beads
- loom needle
- thread
- pattern
- ribbon clamps

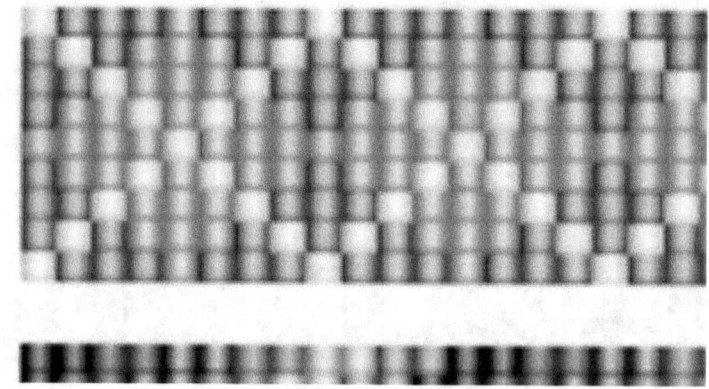

Step 1: Choose a pattern you want to use.

Display it on your phone or another electronic device. You may also print out a design or create one with graph paper.

Step 2: Count the number of beads in a column and then add 1.

This will be the number of strings you will need in your loom.

For example, the green, pink, and white pattern above has 9 beads vertically so we will string 10 rows.

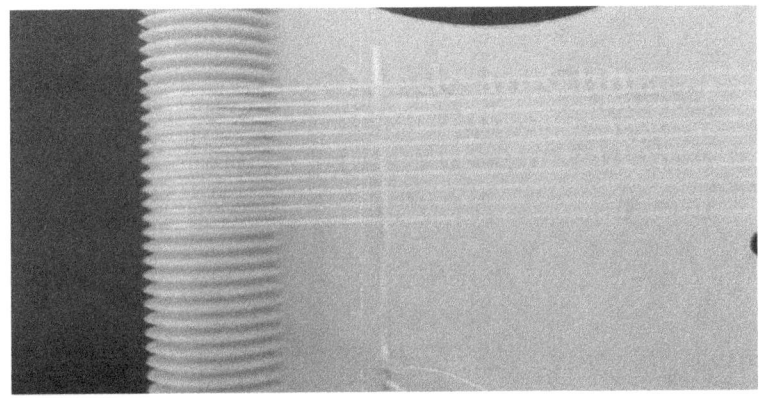

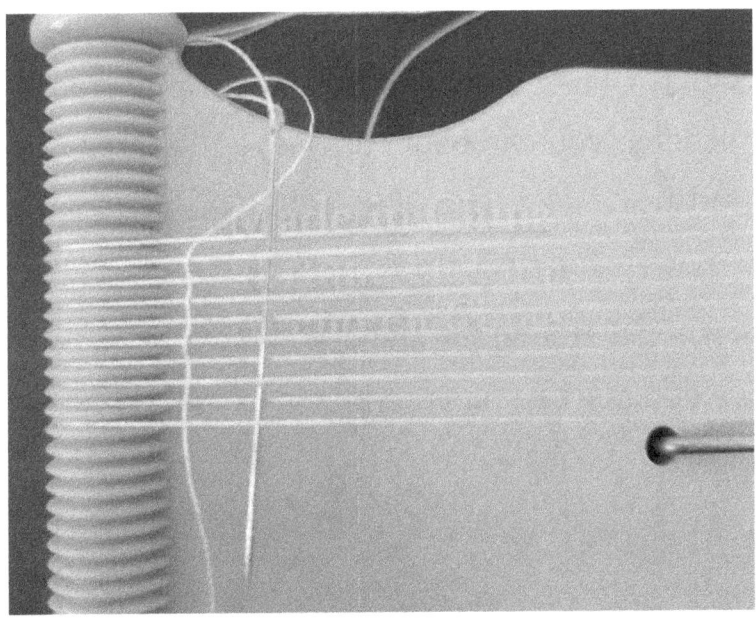

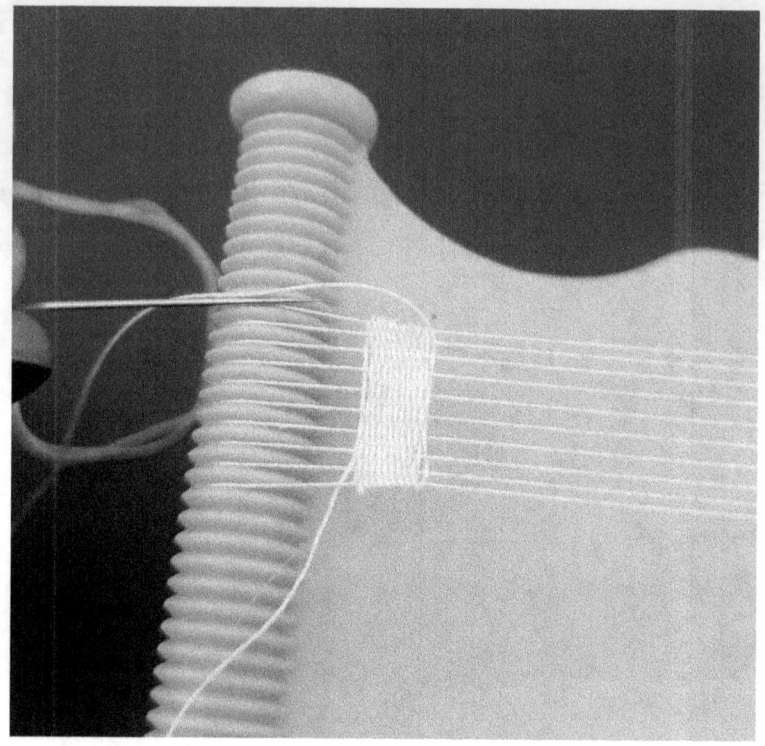

Step 3: Once the loom is strung per manufacturer instructions, you can begin to weave the thread back and forth.

Weave the thread for about a quarter of an inch before you start using your beads to make your pattern.

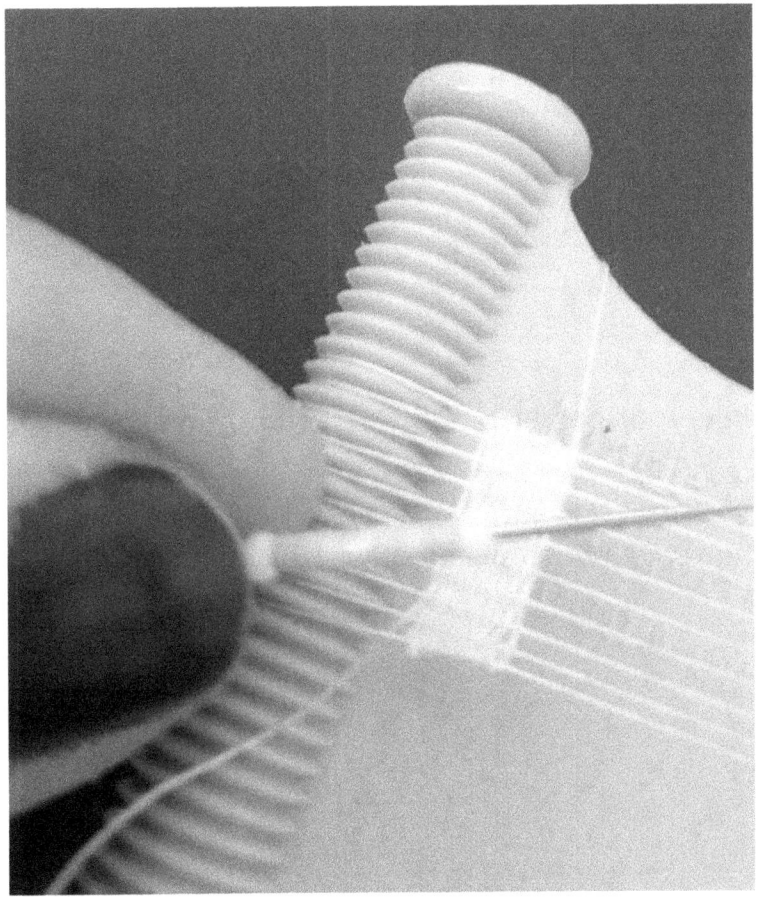

Step 4: Referring to your pattern, string your first row of beads. Run them under the row of threads. Turn your needle and come back to the beads going over the threads.

Step 5: Slide your pattern over one column on your phone, or mark it on your paper.

Craft the next column the same way.

Pick up the beads in the right order, run them under the rows of thread turning your needle.

Go back through your beads going over the threads this time.

Slide your pattern over one column over. Repeat.

There are two ways to finish off your piece:

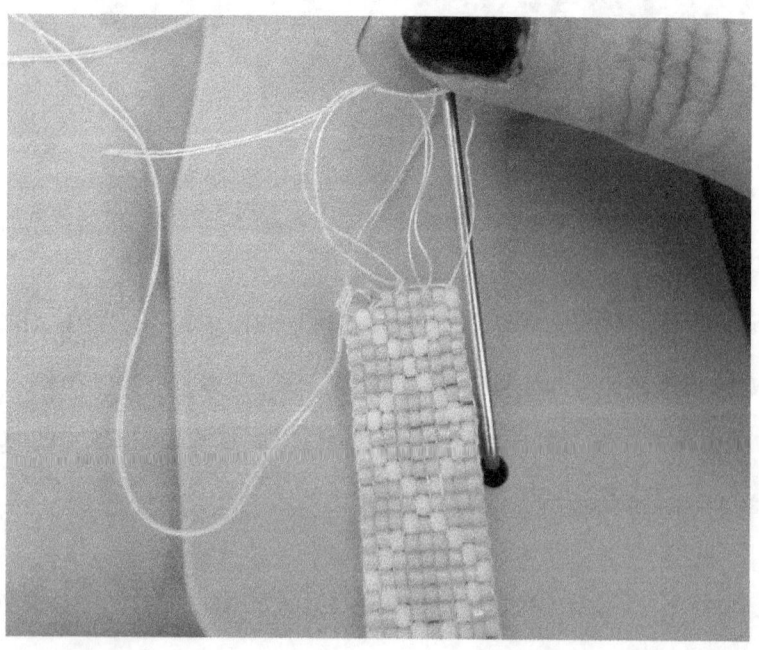

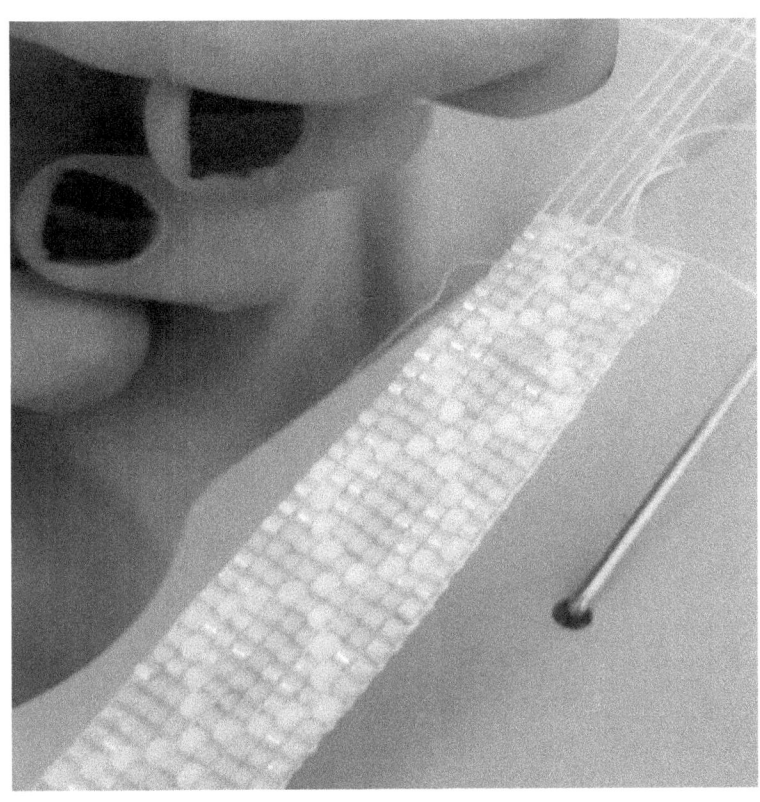
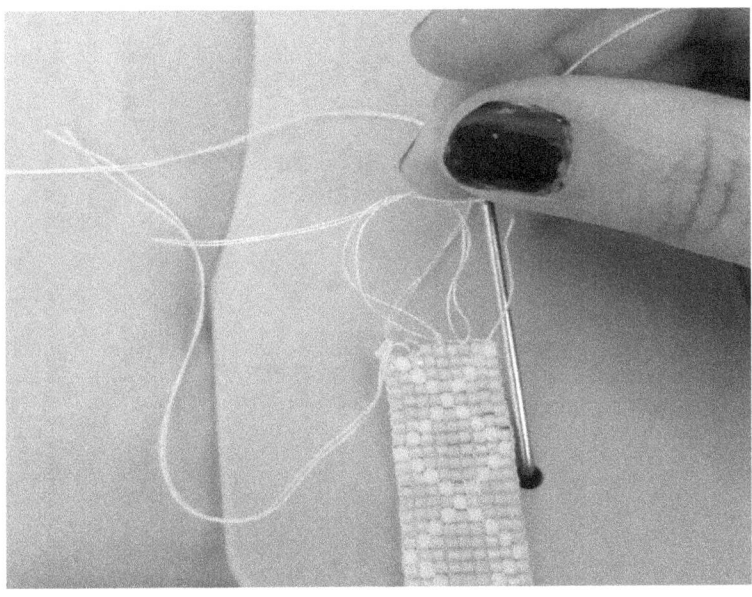

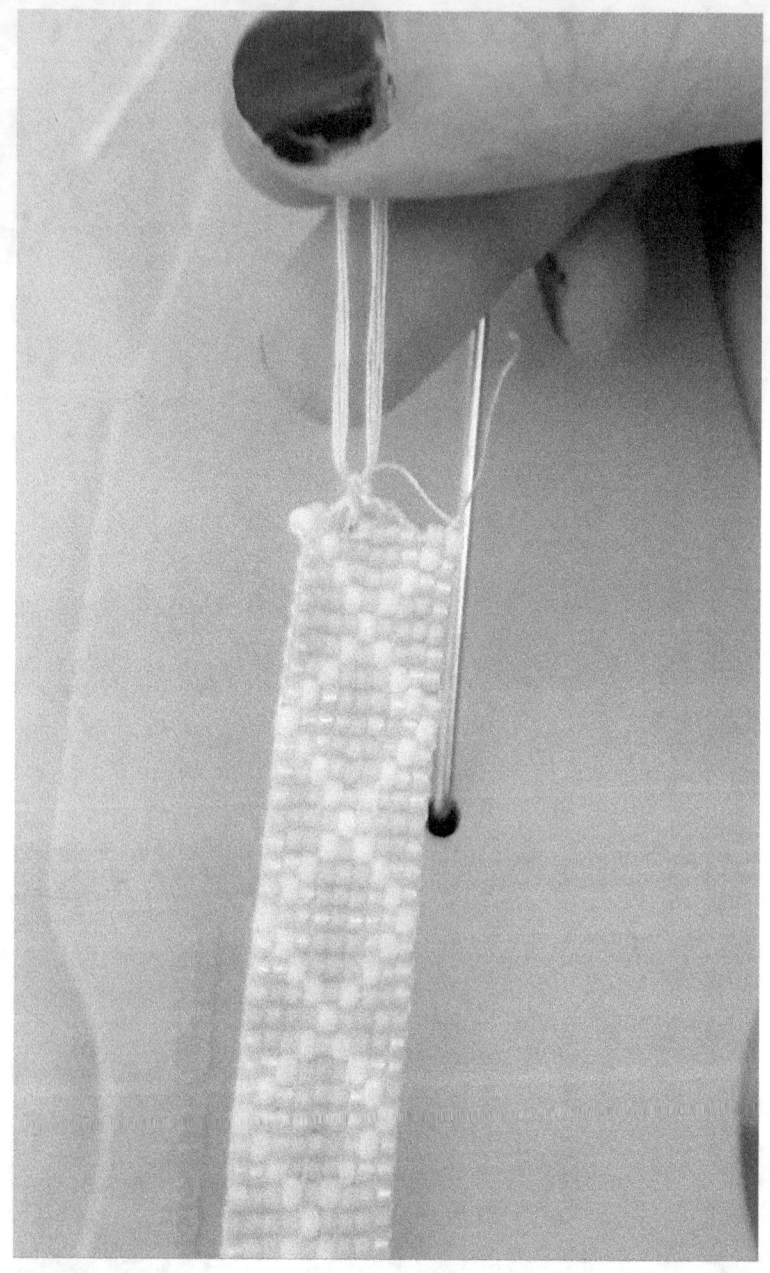

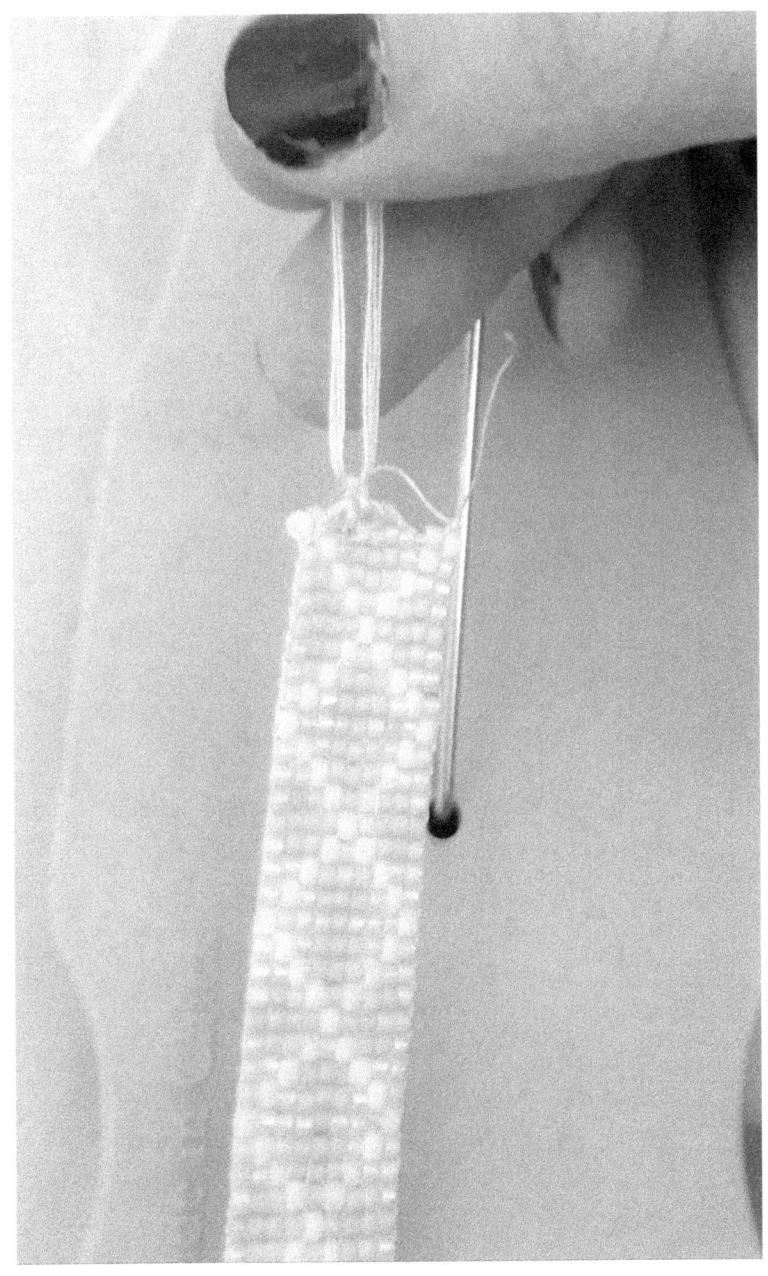

91

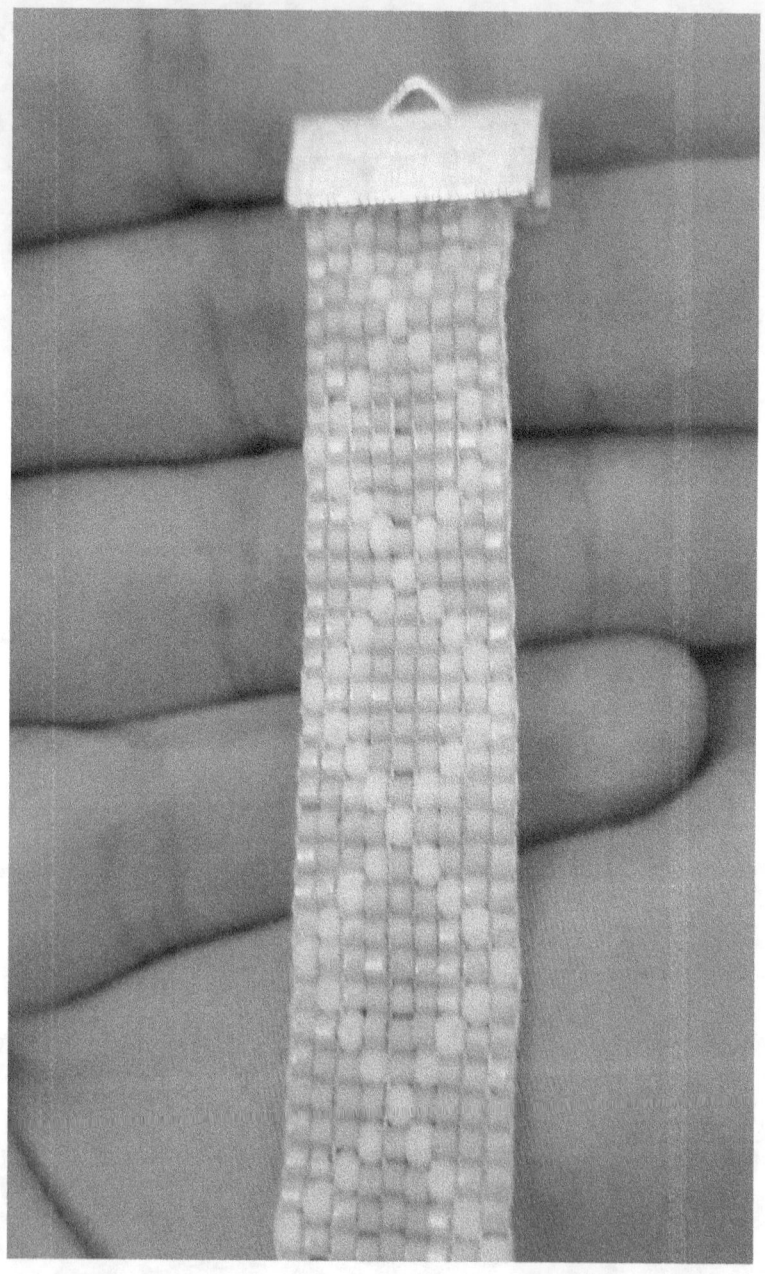

As you start cutting the piece off the loom, tie every two adjacent threads together.

Tie threads 1 and 2 together.

Threads 3 and 4 tie together.

Continue with 5 and 6, 7 and 8, 9 and 10, and so on.

Tie those pairs together until it is well knotted, and you can trim down all the loose threads. Attach a ribbon clamp on the end.

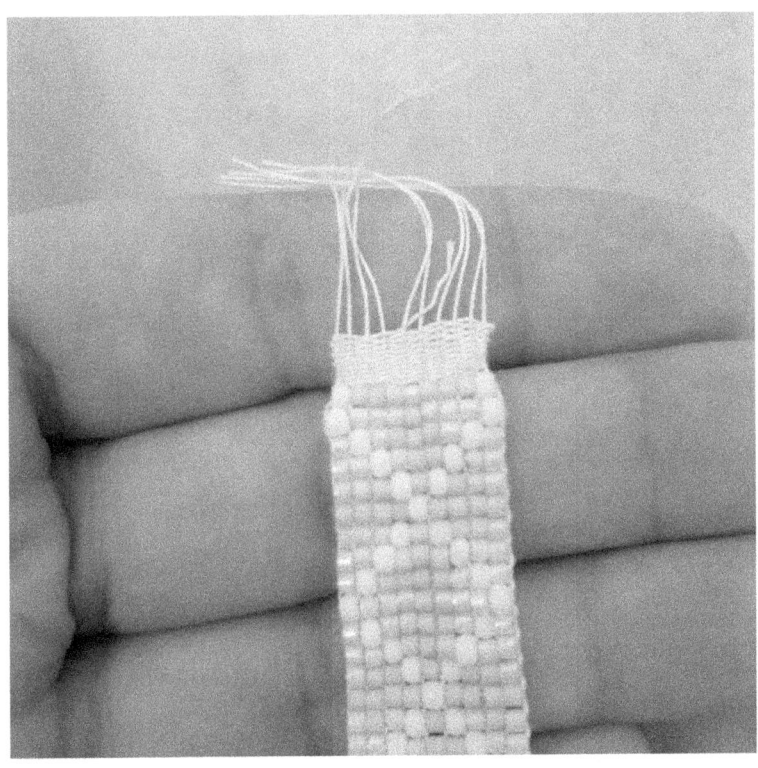

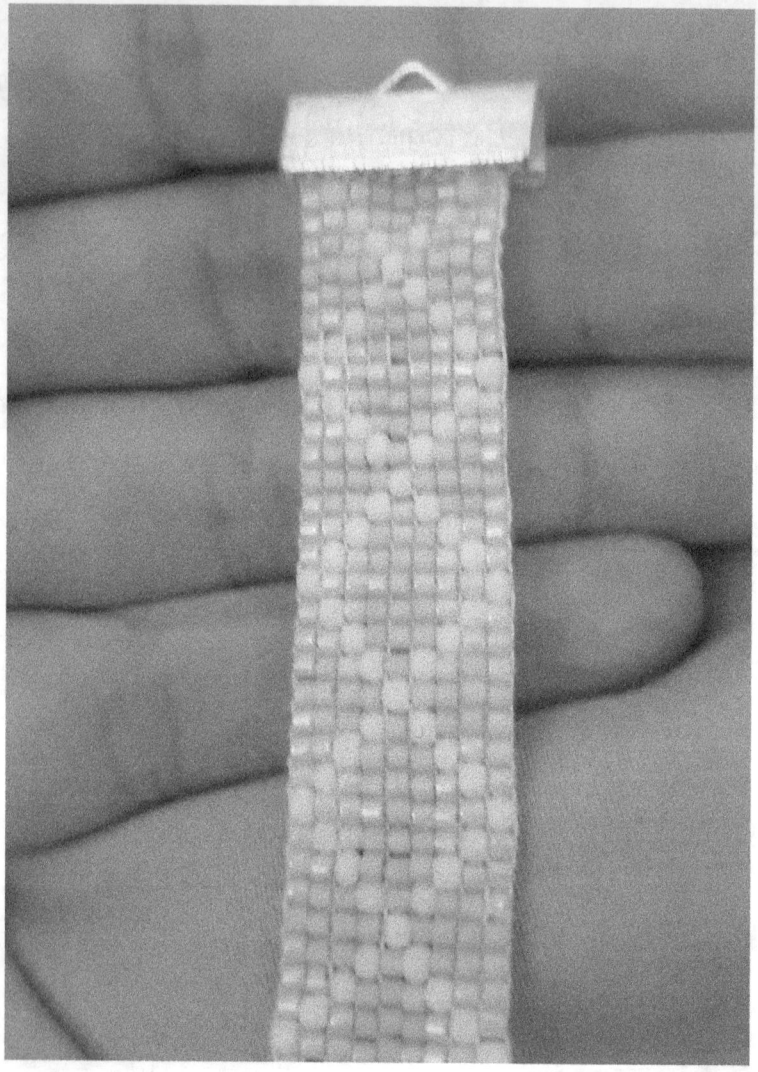

If you wove an extra length of string at the beginning and or at the end, trim the loose strands after you remove it off the loom and put the clamp over the woven part.

Conclusion

Jewelry is a craft that can be expressive, sentimental, personal, and special for a million reasons. Jewelry making is important because you created something with your own two hands.

You put your time, energy, and creativity into something that is unlike anything anyone else owns. You can give someone a gorgeous unique gift that is so personal to them because it came directly from you.

Learning to make a few very basic pieces that can be made with any stone, metal, or charm, in any size or color gives you an endless amount of possibilities.

If this book has touched you, helped you, and inspired you, would you be so kind as to leave a review wherever you purchased this book? I hope to make something out of this crafting hobby, and I appreciate your feedback.

Thank you for reading my book.

Enjoy creating beauty!

www.ingramcontent.com/pod-product-compliance
Lightning Source LLC
Chambersburg PA
CBHW070809220526
45466CB00002B/609